The Student-as-Commuter:
Developing a Comprehensive Institutional Resp

D0220806

by Barbara Jacoby

ASHE-ERIC Higher Education Report 7, 1989

Prepared by

Clearinghouse on Higher Education
The George Washington University

In cooperation with

ASHE

Association for the Study
of Higher Education

Published by

The
George
Washington
University
WASHINGTON DC

School of Education and Human Development
The George Washington University

Jonathan D. Fife, Series Editor

8.96

Cite as

Jacoby, Barbara. *The Student-as-Commuter: Developing a Comprehensive Institutional Response.* ASHE-ERIC Higher Education Report No. 7. Washington, D.C.: School of Education and Human Development, The George Washington University, 1989.

Library of Congress Catalog Card Number 89-063438
ISSN 0884-0040
ISBN 0-9623882-6-2

Managing Editor: Christopher Rigaux
Manuscript Editor: Barbara Fishel/Editech
Cover design by Michael David Brown, Rockville, Maryland

The ERIC Clearinghouse on Higher Education invites individuals to submit proposals for writing monographs for the *ASHE-ERIC Higher Education Report* series. Proposals must include:
1. A detailed manuscript proposal of not more than five pages.
2. A chapter-by-chapter outline.
3. A 75-word summary to be used by several review committees for the initial screening and rating of each proposal.
4. A vita and a writing sample.

ERIC **Clearinghouse on Higher Education**
School of Education and Human Development
The George Washington University
One Dupont Circle, Suite 630
Washington, DC 20036-1183

This publication was prepared partially with funding from the Office of Educational Research and Improvement, U.S. Department of Education, under contract no. ED RI-88-062014. The opinions expressed in this report do not necessarily reflect the positions or policies of OERI or the Department.

EXECUTIVE SUMMARY

Although commuter students account for over 80 percent of today's college students, the residential tradition of American higher education has impeded effective, comprehensive institutional response to their presence. The relationship of commuter students to institutions of higher education has been neither understood nor incorporated into the design of policies, programs, and practices. Too often, it has been assumed erroneously that what has worked for residential students will serve commuter students equally well. More discouragingly, some institutions still barely acknowledge the presence of their commuter students.

Major studies have identified commuters as being at greater risk of attrition, and recent reports calling for reform in higher education have expressed the need to improve the quality of the educational experience for commuter students at all types of institutions. In the current climate, institutions of higher education seek "excellence" and are increasingly held accountable for translating excellence into educational outcomes. Failure to respond effectively and comprehensively to commuter students' needs and educational goals will make excellence impossible to achieve.

Who Are Commuter Students?

Defined as all students who do not live in institution-owned housing, commuter students are an extraordinarily diverse population. Their numbers include full-time students of traditional age who live with their parents, part-time students who live in rental housing near the campus, and adults who have careers and children of their own. The population of commuter students will continue to become more diverse as the number of part-time, adult, and minority students enrolled in higher education increases.

Despite the differences in their backgrounds and educational goals, commuter students share a common core of needs and concerns: issues related to transportation that limit the time they spend on campus, multiple life roles, the importance of integrating their support systems into the collegiate world, and developing a sense of belonging on the campus. Whether they attend a predominantly residential institution or one attended only by commuters, the fact that they commute to college profoundly affects the nature of their educational experience. The term "student-as-commuter" is used to highlight the essential character of the relationship of the commuter student with the institution of higher education.

What Has Impeded the Response of Colleges and Universities to the Student-as-Commuter?

The dominance of the residential tradition of higher education continues to shape the development of policies and practices, even at predominantly commuter institutions. Most administrators and faculty members earned their degrees at traditional residential institutions and tend to impose the values and goals of their own experiences on other educational environments. Administrators often inadvertently believe that commuter students can be served by the substitution of parking lots for residence halls, while maintaining essentially the same curricular and programmatic formats. The focus of much of the preparation, training, and professional work of student personnel practitioners has been on resident students. Residence halls have historically been the site of more student development activity than any other student service. Similarly, the theories and models of student development have been built largely on work with traditional, residential college students.

The research on commuter students is limited in quantity and breadth. Much of it is based on the premise that the residential experience is the normative college experience and that commuters' experiences are somehow less legitimate or less worthy of attention. The findings of the research on commuter students are generally inconsistent and inconclusive.

How Can Administrators and Faculty Develop a Fuller Understanding of the Student-as-Commuter?

A variety of frameworks, theories, and models are useful in understanding the complex nature of the relationship between the student-as-commuter and higher education. The diversity of commuter students and their educational goals requires the use of multiple approaches: human development theories (psychosocial, cognitive, and person-environment), design of the campus ecology/ecosystem, Maslow's hierarchy of needs, mattering, involvement/talent development/integration, transition theory, and family systems. Educators should use the best theoretical frameworks available in the development of institutional policies and practices.

How Can an Institution Assess How Well It Serves Its Commuter Students?

To evaluate whether commuter students' educational goals and needs are being met, each institution must acquire information about its students; its programs, facilities, services, operating assumptions, general climate, and environment; and the nature of students' interactions with the institution. The key variables related to the experience of the student-as-commuter are age, sex, ethnic background, socioeconomic status, finances, employment, family status, living arrangements, distance from campus, modes of transportation, educational aspirations, and academic abilities.

Institutional self-appraisal of the extent to which all students benefit equitably from the institution's offerings should include examination of several aspects from the perspective of the student-as-commuter: mission, image, publications; recruitment, admissions, articulation; funding and fee equity; orientation and transition programs; curriculum and classroom; educational and career planning, academic advising, counseling; faculty/staff development and rewards; sense of community, belonging, recognition; financial aid, on-campus work, experiential learning; cocurricular activities and programs; outreach to significant individuals; community relations; services and facilities; and information and communication.

Once a profile of the student population has been developed and various aspects of the institution have been studied from the perspective of the student-as-commuter, the nature of students' interactions with the institution can be analyzed: retention, satisfaction with the educational experience, achievement of educational goals, use of services and facilities, and participation in various aspects of campus life.

Why Is a Comprehensive Institutional Response Necessary?

Considerable change would be necessary in most institutions to create a high-quality environment for the student-as-commuter. Institutional responses have generally been fragmented attempts to deal with immediate, specific problems rather than long range and comprehensive. Sheer numbers of commuter students have not been sufficient to bring about substantive changes in institutional perspectives, policies, and programs. Nor do institutions attended only by commuters

necessarily provide an experience of equal quality to all
their students.

What Constitutes a Comprehensive Institutional Response to the Student-as-Commuter?

Although it is impossible to provide a recipe or blueprint
for change, it is possible to identify some principal elements
of a comprehensive institutional response:

1. The institution should modify its mission statement, if
   necessary, to express a clear commitment to the quality
   of the educational experience of *all* its students and
   should have that change endorsed by its governing
   board.
2. The president, vice presidents, deans, and all other top
   administrators should frequently and consistently articulate the institution's commitment to the student-as-
   commuter when dealing with faculty, staff, students, the
   governing board, alumni, community members, and
   others.
3. The institution should regularly collect comprehensive
   data about its students and their experiences with the
   institution.
4. Regular evaluation processes should be put in place to
   assess whether the institution's programs, services, facilities, and resources address the needs of all students
   equitably.
5. Steps should be taken to identify and rectify stereotypes
   or inaccurate assumptions held by members of the campus community about commuter students and to ensure
   that commuter students are treated as full members of
   the campus community.
6. Long- and short-range administrative decisions regarding
   resources, policies, and practices should consistently
   include the perspective of the student-as-commuter.
7. In recognition that students' experiences in one segment
   of the institution profoundly affect their experiences
   in other segments and their perceptions of their educational experience as a whole, quality practices should
   be *consistent* throughout the institution.
8. The classroom experience and interactions with faculty
   should be recognized as playing the major roles in deter-

mining the overall quality of commuter students'
education.

9. Curricular and cocurricular offerings should complement
one another, and considerable energy should be directed
to ensure that students understand the interrelationship
of the curriculum and the cocurriculum.

10. Faculty and staff at all levels should be encouraged to
learn more about the theoretical frameworks and models
that lead to a fuller understanding of the student-as-
commuter.

11. Top leadership should actively encourage the various
campus units to work together to implement change
on behalf of the student-as-commuter.

12. Technology should be used to the fullest extent possible
to improve the institution's ability to communicate with
its students and to streamline its administrative processes.

13. Executive officers and members of the governing board
should actively work toward ensuring that commuter
students and commuter institutions are treated fairly in
federal, state, and local decision making (e.g., student
financial aid, institutional funding formulas).

ADVISORY BOARD

Roger G. Baldwin
Assistant Professor of Education
College of William and Mary

Carol M. Boyer
Consultant and Senior Academic Planner
Massachusetts Board of Regents of Higher Education

Ellen Earle Chaffee
Associate Commissioner of Academic Affairs
North Dakota State Board of Higher Education

Martin Finkelstein
Associate Professor of Higher Education Administration
Seton Hall University

Carol Everly Floyd
Associate Vice Chancellor for Academic Affairs
Board of Regents of the Regency Universities System
State of Illinois

George D. Kuh
Professor of Higher Education
Indiana University

Yvonna S. Lincoln
Associate Professor of Higher Education
University of Kansas

Michael A. Olivas
Professor of Law
University of Houston

Richard F. Wilson
Associate Chancellor
University of Illinios

Ami Zusman
Principal Analyst, Academic Affairs
University of California

CONSULTING EDITORS

Leonard L. Baird
Professor
University of Kentucky

James H. Banning
Associate Professor of Psychology
Colorado State University

Trudy W. Banta
Research Professor
University of Tennessee

Margaret J. Barr
Vice Chancellor for Student Affairs
Texas Christian University

Louis W. Bender
Director, State and Regional Higher Education Center
Florida State University

Larry Braskamp
Associate Vice Chancellor for Academic Affairs
University of Illinois

L. Leon Campbell
Provost and Vice President for Academic Affairs
University of Delaware

Darrell Clowes
Associate Professor of Education
Viginia Tech

Susan Cohen
Associate, Project for Collaborative Learning
Lesley College

John W. Creswell
Professor and Lilly Project Director
University of Nebraska

Mary E. Dilworh
Director, Research and Information Services
ERIC Clearinghouse on Teacher Education

James A. Eison
Director, Center for Teaching and Learning
Southeast Missouri State University

Lawrence Erickson
Professor and Coordinator of Reading and Language Studies
Southern Illinois University

Valerie French
Professor of History
American University

J. Wade Gilley
Senior Vice President
George Mason University

Milton Greenberg
Provost
American University

Judith Dozier Hackman
Associate Dean
Yale University

Brian L. Hawkins
Vice President for Computing and Information Sciences
Brown University

Oscar T. Lenning
Vice President for Academic Affairs
Robert Wesleyan College

James W. Lyons
Dean of Student Affairs
Stanford University

Judith B. McLaughlin
Research Associate on Education and Sociology
Harvard University

Andrew T. Masland
Judicial/Public Safety Market Manager
Digital Equipment Corporation

Jeanne Mihikins
Director, Commuter Student Affairs Office
The Ohio State University

Christopher B. Morris
Director of Athletics
Davidson College

Yolanda T. Moses
Vice President for Academic Affairs
California State University

Michael T. Nettles
Senior Research Scientist
Educational Testing Service

Elizabeth M. Nuss
Executive Director
National Association of Student Personnel Administrators

Jeffrey H. Orleans
Executive Director
Council of Ivy Group Presidents

Wayne Otto
Professor of Curriculum and Instruction
University of Wisconsin

James J. Rhatigan
Vice President for Student Affairs
Wichita State University

John E. Roueche
Professor and Director
Community College Leadership Program
Sid W. Richardson Regents Chair
University of Texas

Mary Ellen Sheridan
Director of Sponsored Programs Administration
Ohio State University

William F. Stier, Jr.
Professor and Director of Intercollegiate Athletics
State University of New York at Brockport

Betty Taylor
Dean of the Graduate School
Lesley College

Reginald Wilson
Senior Scholar
American Council on Education

CONTENTS

FOREWORD

The student-as-commuter is used in this report to signify not only difference in domicile and transportation from the traditional residential student but also to bring greater meaning to cultural, sociological, and psychological differences. It also is used to emphasize the concept that "commuter students" are not a homogeneous mass: They include multiple variations based on age, race, income, educational goals, marital status, and the like that greatly influence why they have chosen to study at a particular institution yet find it to their advantage to not live at the institution.

It has been more than 25 years since higher education began to accept its role in promoting equal educational opportunity. A prime example of this role is the willingness of institutions to accept nonresidential students. The irony is that while administrators have effectively accepted students-as-commuters, the faculty have accepted them to a degree and facilities have been modified only slightly to accommodate the special needs of the student-as-commuter. As is repeatedly demonstrated in this report, the major difference in the minds of the faculty between residential students and students who commute is where they sleep and how they get to class. Consideration for students' disposal time, accessibility to libraries and laboratories, and the development of strong peer support groups are often overlooked.

Demographic data indicates that the percentage of students who commute is not likely to decrease in the near future. In fact, evidence strongly suggests that the percentage will increase. With an increasing emphasis from funding sources, whether state legislators or a private board of trustees, on assessment of an institution's effectiveness in achieving its educational mission, institutions will be forced to take a closer look at students-as-commuters.

This report by Barbara Jacoby, director of the Office of Commuter Affairs and the National Clearinghouse for Commuter Programs at the University of Maryland, reviews the knowledge we have about students-as-commuters in depth. What is of particular interest is that once Dr. Jacoby has established a firm base in the literature for commuter students and developed a set of frameworks, theories, and models, she clearly outlines how institutions can assess their effectiveness with their commuting students. The concluding recommendations for developing a comprehensive institutional response to the student-as-commuter will greatly help institutions develop a more effective approach to these students.

Whether the result of reactions that were based on academic tradition or the majority of the faculty's and academic leaders' status once were residential students, the general approach that institutions have for students-as-commuters is inadequate. This report clearly represents the concise description of the problem and specific steps that will help institutions develop greater sensitivity to the needs of these students.

Jonathan D. Fife
Series Editor, Professor of Higher Education, and
Director, ERIC Clearinghouse on Higher Education
School of Education and Human Development
The George Washinton University

ACKNOWLEDGMENTS

I am indebted to many persons without whose support and hard work this report would never have been written. First, I thank the staff of the National Clearinghouse for Commuter Programs and the Office of Commuter Affairs at the University of Maryland at College Park. Their enthusiasm for this project and their dedication to serving commuter students have been a constant and essential inspiration to me.

Peggy Barr, Jeanne Likins, Sylvia Stewart, Deborah Taub, and Martha Baer Wilmes were kind enough to read the initial draft and to share their honest thoughts with me. Four anonymous reviewers then read the much-revised manuscript and offered useful suggestions. Dr. Likins spent many hours with this report in various stages, and I cannot imagine what it would be like without her encouragement and assistance. Any remaining weaknesses in this report are solely my responsibility.

Bob Nedwich served as an excellent—and relentless—researcher. Anita Ahalt and her staff did superb work in the preparation of the manuscript. Chris Rigaux, as managing editor of the report series, was helpful and supportive from the beginning of the lengthy process of writing and revising.

With deep appreciation, I acknowledge the loving patience of my husband, Steve Jacoby, who has lived and breathed this project along with me. Steve, too, read the manuscript and it is better as a result of his incisive remarks. He and my wonderful parents are always my "fans."

I thank "those who went before," the individuals whose work with and writings about commuter students have served as a firm foundation for current endeavors. It is with respect and affection that I salute my caring and tireless colleagues who are members of the National Clearinghouse for Commuter Programs, ACPA's Commission XVII (Commuter Programs), and NASPA's Commuter Network. I hope this report will live up to their expectations and be of use to them. I wish them all the best in their never-ending work to enhance the college experience of commuter students at their institutions.

COMMUTER STUDENTS AND THE STUDENT-AS-COMMUTER

Commuter students—those who do not live in institution-owned housing—account for over 80 percent of the students in American colleges and universities today. Nevertheless, the residential tradition of higher education continues to impede effective institutional response to their presence. Educators have assumed that commuters are like resident students except that they live off campus and that curricular and cocurricular offerings are equally appropriate for all students. This assumption has not served commuter students well. Several major studies have identified commuters as particularly high risks for attrition (Astin 1975, 1977, 1985; Chickering 1974; Tinto 1987). Recent books and articles focusing specifically on commuter students (Jacoby and Burnett 1986b; Jacoby and Girrell 1981; Stewart 1983) and a series of reports regarding higher education in general (Boyer 1987; Study Group 1984; Task Group 1988) have emphasized the need to enhance the quality of the educational experience for commuter students.

Several major studies have identified commuters as particularly high risks for attrition.

Commuter students attend virtually every institution of higher education. Their numbers include full-time students who live at home with their parents as well as fully employed adults who live with their spouses and/or children and attend college part time. Commuters may reside near the campus or far away; they commute by car, public transportation, walking, and bicycle. They may represent a small minority of students at a private, residential liberal arts college or the entire population of a community college or urban institution.

The problem of defining commuter students has, among other factors, slowed the development of a comprehensive understanding of the largest student population in higher education. Confusion has existed as to whether adult students should be included in the definition of "commuter." What about students who live in rental housing adjacent to the campus? And students at community colleges and urban institutions that have no housing—are they *commuters* or are they just *students?* In addition to vague definitions, commuters are not present on campus all at the same time and thus cannot be observed as a group. Because they do not identify with one another as commuters and often have limited involvement with the institution, they do not represent themselves as a strong constituency group.

In the last decade or so, the definition of commuter students as all students who do not live in institution-owned housing has emerged as the preferred one (Stewart and Rue

1983), and the National Clearinghouse for Commuter Programs, a number of key professional associations within higher education, and the authors of the recent reports calling for reform in higher education have adopted this definition. Despite the diverse nature of the population, the use of the broad definition of commuter student promotes recognition of the substantial core of needs and concerns all commuter students share. It also encourages institutions to regard their population of commuter students as an aggregate for the purpose of ensuring that they receive their fair share of attention and resources.

The Increasing Diversity of Students in Higher Education

American higher education is characterized by the diversity of its institutions and its students. Predicted declines in enrollment in the late 1970s and 1980s have not occurred because of the attendance of an increasingly diverse body of students. As a result:

> *The average student today is much different from the stereotype of a full-time student 18–22 years old, financed mostly by parents, and living away from home: This description now applies to less than a fifth of those enrolled in colleges and universities* (Commission on National Challenges in Higher Education 1988, p. 16).

Fifty-four percent of all college students live off campus, not with a parent or parents, while 27 percent live with a parent or parents (U.S. Department of Education 1988, p. 10).

The percentage of traditional-age, full-time residential students will continue to decline as we move toward the middle 1990s. The number of high school graduates is expected to decrease by 25 percent by 1994, and the decline of suburban, 18- to 24-year-old, full-time, white, middle-class students will be felt most heavily (Hodgkinson 1985).

At the same time, enrollments of adults and part-time students have increased dramatically. Over 40 percent of college students are 25 years of age or older (United Way of America 1987). By 1992, more than one-half of the total college enrollment will be over 25, and 20 percent will be over 35 (Hodgkinson 1985). Related to the trend in ages as well as to the escalating costs of higher education, two-fifths of the more than 12 million individuals enrolled in colleges and universities in 1985 attended part time. By 1990, over half of all students will be enrolled part time (Commission on National Challenges 1988; Keller 1983).

The composition of students in higher education will continue to change in other ways. Over 50 percent of all college students are women. Enrollments of American Indian, Asian, African-American, and Hispanic students have risen substantially in the last 20 years—although in some cases not at a rate rapid enough to reflect their proportion of the American population. Projections indicate that by 2000 more than 40 percent of public school students in the United States will be minority children and that the college-age population in that year will be one-third minority (Hodgkinson 1985).

The vast majority of the students in these increasing populations are and will continue to be commuters for reasons of age, life-style, family circumstances, and financial necessity. Students with spouses, children, and/or full-time jobs are not likely to live in residence halls—nor are many students from ethnic cultures that place the highest value on the maintenance of the family unit (Wright 1987b). And, given that high proportions of minority and low-income students attend community colleges and urban institutions that generally do not have residence facilities, it is clear that the opportunity "to live in a residence hall is not equally allocated among American college students by ethnicity and income level" (Astin 1985, p. 91).

Although adult, part-time, and minority students enroll more heavily in community colleges and urban four-year institutions, the approximately 10 million commuter students are distributed across all types of institutions. An extrapolation from the results of a 1982 study of student housing by the American Council on Education shows a distribution of *full-time* commuter students as follows: all institutions, 61 percent commuters; public universities, 68 percent; public four-year colleges, 66 percent; public two-year colleges, 76 percent; private universities, 58 percent; private four-year colleges, 41 percent; and private two-year colleges, 50 percent (Stewart and Rue 1983). While these percentages reflect full-time students only, it has been noted that over 40 percent of all students attend *part time*. Thus, if part-time enrollments had been included in this study, the percentages would be much higher. The study also indicates that more than one-third of

all institutions had no housing for students and could be considered 100 percent commuter campuses (Andersen and Atelsek 1982).

A Useful Categorization of Commuter Students

Because the population of commuter students incorporates a tremendous diversity of students who bring to higher education a broad range of goals and needs, it is useful to distinguish several types of commuter students. One categorization is based on three variables: (1) dependence or independence in living arrangements, (2) traditional or nontraditional age, and (3) full- or part-time enrollment (Stewart and Rue 1983). Dependent students live at home with parents or other close relatives who assume parental responsibilities; independent students live alone, with peers, or with their own families. Commuters of traditional college age share many of the developmental needs of their residential counterparts. Older commuters may be returning to school after a break in their education, employed in a career position, and with spouses and children. Commuters' attendance patterns often reflect their other roles and commitments and affect the degree to which they may concentrate on their education.

The interactions among these three variables yield eight distinct subgroups of commuter students, listed in table 1 with examples of students who might fit into each category. The number of commuter students in each subgroup varies considerably from institution to institution. A later section ("Institutional Self-Assessment") addresses the process by which an institution should assess its particular population of commuter students.

The Student-as-Commuter: Common Needs and Concerns

No matter what commuter students' educational goals are, where they live, or what type of institution they attend, the fact that they commute to college profoundly influences the nature of their educational experience. For residential students, home and campus are synonymous; for commuter students, the campus is a place to visit, sometimes for very short periods (Likins 1988).

To denote the essential character of the relationship of the commuter student with the institution of higher education,

TABLE 1

A CATEGORIZATION OF COMMUTER STUDENTS

Category	Example
• Dependent, traditional, full time	An 18-year-old freshman who lives at home because of family reasons or financial constraints
• Dependent, nontraditional, full time	A divorcee with children who has returned to her parents' home so she can attend college full time
• Dependent, nontraditional, part time	A veteran who lives with parents or other relatives and attends part time
• Dependent, traditional, part time	A 19-year-old student who lives at home and works full time
• Independent, traditional, full time	An international student who attends full time with full support of the home government and lives in a rented room
• Independent, nontraditional, full time	A retiree who has returned to school full time and is supported by a pension
• Independent, nontraditional, part time	An adult with a full-time position and a family who takes courses to enhance a career
• Independent, traditional, part time	A 20-year-old student who lives in a rented apartment, works to support herself, and attends college part time

the term "student-as-commuter" is used in this report. Although the students themselves are extraordinarily diverse, a common core of needs and concerns of the student-as-commuter can be identified (Wilmes and Quade 1986):

• *Transportation issues:* The most obvious concerns commuter students share are those related to transportation to campus: parking, traffic, fixed transportation schedules, inclement weather, maintaining a car, transportation costs, and finding alternative means of transportation. No matter the mode, commuting is demanding in terms of time and energy. Commuter students frequently concentrate their classes into blocks and have little free time to spend on campus. Convenience in curricular offerings, services, and programs is of paramount importance.
• *Multiple life roles:* For young and old alike, being a student is only one of several important and demanding roles. Most

commuter students work; many have responsibilities for managing households and for caring for children, siblings, or older relatives. By necessity, commuters select their campus involvements carefully. It is critical that complete information about campus options and opportunities reaches them in a timely manner. The *relative value* of an activity is a major factor in their decision to participate.

- *Integrating support systems:* The support networks for commuter students generally exist off campus: parents, siblings, spouses, children, employers, coworkers, and friends in the community. Each semester, students must negotiate with family, employers, and friends to establish priorities and responsibilities and to allot time. These negotiations are more difficult if significant others have no knowledge about the challenges and opportunities of higher education. It is important for institutions to provide opportunities for these individuals to learn about and to participate appropriately in the life of the campus.

- *Developing a sense of belonging:* Commuter students often lack a sense of belonging, of "feeling wanted" by the institution. Some institutions fail to provide basic facilities, such as lockers and lounges, which enable students to put down roots. In many cases, institutions do not provide adequate opportunities for commuter students to develop relationships with faculty, staff, and other students. Individuals rarely feel connected to a place where they have no significant relationships. Students who do not have a sense of belonging complain about the "supermarket" or "filling station" nature of their collegiate experience.

This report discusses why the relationship of the student-as-commuter to the institution of higher education has not been fully understood or incorporated into the design of policies, programs, and practices and how colleges and universities can bring about positive changes in this regard. The following section examines the residential nature of the history and tradition of American higher education and its persistent ramifications. The following two sections review the literature on commuting students and present a selection of theories and models to increase understanding of the student-as-commuter. The next section addresses how colleges and universities can assess their own commuter students and how well all their students are served by various aspects of the institution. And the final section describes the development of a comprehensive institutional response to the educational goals and needs of the student-as-commuter.

THE EFFECTS OF THE RESIDENTIAL TRADITION

Residential History of American Higher Education

Residence halls have been an essential aspect of American higher education since its earliest days. Colonial colleges adopted the residential system from the English model (Eddy 1977; Rudolph 1962; Schneider 1977; Williamson and Biggs 1975). Providing on-campus housing was usually one of the first priorities of the early colleges, for reasons of necessity and philosophy. The necessity arose because colleges were generally located in isolated settings or where boarding facilities were insufficient. Philosophically, it was believed that young men preparing for the clergy (who were the earliest college students) should live in settings where their behavior could be monitored (Delworth, Hanson, and Associates 1980; Eddy 1977).

The residential model of higher education has become "a tradition so fundamental, so all-encompassing, that to call it merely a tradition is to undervalue it. For what is involved here is nothing less than a way of life, the collegiate way" (Rudolph 1962, p. 87).

> *The collegiate way is the notion that a curriculum, a library, a faculty, and students are not enough to make a college. It is an adherence to the residential scheme of things. It is respectful of quiet rural settings, dependent on dormitories, committed to dining halls, permeated by paternalism. . . . Not to have the collegiate way would have required cities— cities that could offer up sufficient numbers of students and that could find rooms in their attics and in their basements for students attracted to the college from the surrounding countryside. In the absence of cities and knowing the English pattern, the founders of Harvard and other colonial colleges naturally subscribed to the collegiate way. By the time that the colleges in Philadelphia and New York were under way, the collegiate pattern was not a necessity, for there were cities. But by then what had been a necessity had become a tradition, and from then on the founders of American colleges either adhered to the tradition or clumsily sought a new rationale* (Rudolph 1962, pp. 87–88).

Such students were young, advantaged, and attended day classes full time.

Throughout the tremendous growth and diversification of higher education following the Civil War, it was "taken for granted that colleges provide housing for students" (Schneider 1977, p. 126). The initial concept of the dormitory as a place where students could be supervised and controlled gradually shifted toward an educational focus. Around the turn of the 20th century, Princeton, Harvard, and the University of Chicago developed house plans that were influential in propagating the philosophy that residence living is a key factor in the education of students (Arbuckle 1953; Delworth, Hanson, and Associates 1980; Williamson and Biggs 1975). Shortly after World War I, the student personnel movement became more formally organized, and residence halls were regarded as sites for personal and social, as well as educational, development (Williamson and Biggs 1975).

As colleges and universities, especially those in the public sector, expanded rapidly after World War II, construction of residence halls boomed. Simultaneously, student personnel professionals continued to concentrate the majority of their efforts on the development of intellectual, cultural, and extracurricular programs in the residence halls, despite a huge influx of veterans and other "new" students who commuted to college.

In the 20 years between 1955 and 1974, the number of college students more than tripled, expanding from 2.5 million to 8.8 million (Keller 1983). To handle this explosion of students, the United States doubled its college and university facilities, adding hundreds of new two-year community colleges. Because only 2.3 million students were placed in institution-controlled housing in 1980, when the number of college students was over 12 million (Andersen and Atelsek 1982), the vast majority of the growth in the student population was the result of commuter students. Throughout the 1960s and 1970s, however, the response to this dramatic increase in the number of commuter students was construction of new colleges and universities and expansion of existing ones, "copying with only minor wrinkles the models of the past" (Chickering 1974, p. 1). "Staffing patterns, scheduling arrangements, annual cycles of activity, and areas of expertise for student personnel professionals continued to be established for traditional-age, full-time, mostly on-campus" students (Schlossberg, Lynch, and Chickering 1989, p. 228). Ironically, it was true in community colleges and in 100 percent commuter, four-year institutions as well.

As the distinctive character of American higher education evolved, Rudolph's "collegiate way" became a fully developed undergraduate culture. "College life" (described in detail by Horowitz 1987), has flourished in four-year residential institutions since the late 18th century. Fraternal organizations and intercollegiate athletics formed the basis of college life; alcohol, parties, sex, and campus activities rounded out the picture. Novels like Fitzgerald's *This Side of Paradise* and Weller's *Not to Eat, Not for Love* vividly captured the essence of college life. College life, however, never included all students. "Outsiders" have always existed, and commuters have generally fallen into this group. Most outsiders neither embraced nor fought college life; they mainly ignored it (Horowitz 1987).

Even as the number of commuter students continues to increase in comparison to resident students, the popular media abound with portrayals of the collegiate experience in terms of traditional-age students who leave home immediately after high school to go away to college, live on campus, and attend college full time. Books and films like *Love Story, Animal House, Breaking Away,* and *Good-bye, Columbus* have become part of American contemporary culture. Each fall television and newspapers feature stories about students packing up their cars, saying good-bye to their parents, moving into residence halls, and meeting their new roommates.

The dominance of the residential tradition of higher education continues to exert tremendous, albeit often subtle, influence on the experience of commuter students. Colleges and universities regard themselves (and rightly so) as the keepers of the proud traditions of higher education:

> *You can still hear the old saw on many campuses, "We don't do things that way," implying that the present policies and procedures are rooted in the past and its leader traditions, and that this is how it should forever be* (Keller 1983, p. 67).

Yet this preservationist attitude often leads to failure to recognize the profound changes that have occurred in the population of college students who are not represented in the traditions of the past.

It is not only the tradition-rich residential institutions that have failed to respond to the increasing numbers and diversity

The dominance of the residential tradition of higher education continues to exert tremendous . . . influence on the experience of commuter students.

of commuter students. While some predominantly commuter institutions have provided courses during evening and weekend hours, large parking lots and access to public transportation, and lounges and eating facilities:

> . . .there are no significant responses to the special backgrounds of many commuting students, no attempts to deal with the difficulties they have in discovering and connecting with academic programs and extracurricular activities suitable to them, and no solutions to the difficulties they face in building new relationships with students and faculty members and with the institution itself (Chickering 1974, p. 3).

Administrators have accepted "the simplistic solution of eliminating the residential facilities and maintaining essentially the same educational programs and processes" (Chickering 1974, p. 3). Commuter campuses "are administered with little distinction from their counterparts" (Lindahl 1967, p. 10). Surprisingly few differences have been found between student services at commuter institutions and traditional residential institutions (Jones and Damron 1987). Urban institutions suffer from "an overvaluing of traditional ways at the expense of local community needs" (Richardson and Bender 1985, p. 7), and community colleges have adopted "the same basic procedures, facilities, and approaches to teaching and learning that had characterized four-year colleges and universities since the turn of the century" (Chickering 1974, p. 1).

Attitudes of Faculty and Administrators
The majority of today's faculty members earned their undergraduate and graduate degrees at traditional residential institutions (Grobman 1980; Lindquist 1981; Lynton and Ellman 1987). The time-honored system of instruction with 120 credit hours of coursework earned between the ages of 18 and 22 is a formula that is ingrained in faculty well before they take charge of a classroom (Lindquist 1981). Most faculty members seem to expect the institutions where they teach to be similar to the institutions they attended and therefore impose the values and goals of those institutions (e.g., total immersion in the intellectual community) on their new environments (Grobman 1980; Lynton and Ellman 1987). The image of a residential institution is often "perpetuated by the memories

and experiences of faculty, staff, alumni, and others long after a shift to a predominantly commuter student population has taken place" (Stewart 1983, p. 1).

Many administrators and faculty have still not adjusted to the fact that students frequently attend part time and have responsibilities for jobs and families (Educational Facilities Laboratories 1977; McLaughlin 1985). It may be difficult for some professors to accept what may seem to be a lesser academic commitment. "Most of today's professors and administrators have acquired, from their own experience as students, deeply rooted ideas about higher learning that may hinder their ability to respond to new circumstances" (Lindquist 1981, p. 733). Faculty sometimes shun assignments to an urban campus (Richardson and Bender 1985), while others "look down on 'subway circuit' students and treat them as second-class citizens" (Educational Facilities Laboratories 1977, p. 7). "Administrators may not be able to shake themselves of the notion that, if students really cared about a campus, they would live on it" (Stewart and Rue 1983, p. 4).

Common misperceptions and myths persist about commuter students and reflect outdated or inaccurate perspectives. One of the most prevalent is to think of traditional-age students who live with their parents near the college as "townies" because in the past, such students were admitted under a different set of standards and were not expected to be full members of the college community. In a similar vein, another stereotype of commuters is immature and unable to break away from parental control. In contrast, the protest era of the 1960s gave rise to the perception of students who lived off campus as "trouble makers" who rebelled against or were unable to conform to on-campus living. And commuters, both traditional age and older, continue to be thought of as apathetic or uninterested in campus life (Stewart and Rue 1983).

Student Personnel and Student Development
As mentioned earlier, the roots of the student personnel profession are in the residence halls. It remains true that residence halls are the largest single employer of student affairs staff, and residence halls have historically been the site of more student development than any other single student service (Eddy 1977). Student personnel graduate preparation programs tend to be located at institutions where student populations are mainly of traditional age, where large residence

hall programs exist, and where policies, services, and programs focus on 18- to 22-year-old, full-time students (Jacoby 1987). Professional in-service workshops are geared primarily toward "serving the resident students' particular needs" (Likins 1984). As a result, most cocurricular programming, even in commuter institutions, is "patterned after and/or is focused on the residential student" (Hardy and Williamson 1974, p. 47). Staff members find it easier to communicate with resident students and may not reach out to commuter students because they feel that commuters are beyond their reach. A similar problem exists when staff view commuters as primarily evening or part-time students who are not interested in or do not need student services (Stewart and Rue 1983).

Since the 1960s, theories and models of student development have increasingly become the basis for the education and practice of student personnel administrators. The models and theories have been built largely on research on white, middle-class, traditional-age students at predominantly private, four-year residential colleges, however (Barr et al. 1988; Stodt 1982). No "systematically organized body of research and theory directly addresses the commuting student, his experiences, and the educational outcomes [that] flow from them" (Chickering 1974, p. 137). While substantial research documents the "powerful contribution to personal development and intellectual competence made by residence on a college campus," no similar work exists regarding the commuting experience (Chickering 1974, p. xi).

Largely because residence on campus has been considered the normative experience of college students, it has been assumed that commuter students' development would parallel that of residents or that commuters' environments do not facilitate development. This situation is unfortunate, because the knowledge gained from studying commuter students in all their diversity and complexity would enhance and expand our notions of college students' development (Knefelkamp and Stewart 1983). Speaking of his own research on student development published in 1969, Chickering acknowledged that he had made several assumptions that turned out to be erroneous, including that most students would be of traditional age and would live on campus (1984).

The lack of models of student development for commuter students has led to a plethora of research analyzing commuters in terms of their differences from resident students. Based on the models developed and normed on resident students, much of this research has considered these differences to be deficits rather than simply differences. Areas of maturation and growth likely to be more highly developed by commuter students (e.g., vocational choice and instrumental autonomy) have not been appropriately incorporated into theoretical frameworks or models (Knefelkamp and Stewart 1983).

In numerous ways, the collegiate experience is equated with the residential experience in the minds of educators. This misconception has profoundly affected the design and development of institutions and programs, and it continues to color the way in which faculty and administrators perceive commuter students and their educational goals. The following section describes the effects of higher education's residential tradition on the literature regarding commuter students.

THE LITERATURE ON COMMUTER STUDENTS

Although the body of literature about commuter students is limited in quantity and breadth, it is difficult to synthesize. It is possible, however, to distinguish five waves of literature, each of which evinces common characteristics, themes, and attitudes. The notion of waves is used to connote the sequential but not absolutely discrete nature of the phases in the literature about commuter students. In addition, the use of the analogy acknowledges the presence of undertows created by contradictory data and conflicting themes.

The First Wave: Narrow Scope, Negative Images

The literature on the commuter student that preceded the work of Chickering and Astin in the mid-1970s consisted mainly of relatively brief descriptive studies of very limited scope. Most of these studies focused on a traditional-age, full-time, often single-sex population at a particular time at one institution. They relied primarily on descriptive or survey data and self-report. The research was usually based on small samples, often with low rates of response. For the most part, commuters were compared with resident students. Although the majority of the studies were conducted at four-year, predominantly residential institutions, some attention was paid to commuter institutions.

In this first wave of research, investigators concentrated heavily on the areas of academic success and mental health. They showed considerable interest in determining whether place of residence affected academic performance and whether commuters suffered more mental and emotional problems than students who lived on campus. The body of literature is problematic and inconclusive, because researchers who claimed to be studying the same problem frequently did not examine the same variables, employ the same methods, or select comparable samples.

Commuters versus residents: Contradictory findings

Beginning with the earliest research that attempted to relate place of residence to academic success, the results of the studies contradict one another. One researcher stated that students who lived in residence halls ranked above "home," fraternity, and rooming-house students on several measures of academic performance (Walker 1935), while another found that where students lived had little bearing on scholastic achievement (Van Alstine 1942, cited in Reeve 1966). Several studies in the 1960s and early 1970s revealed few differences on academic variables between commuter and resident students (Baird 1969; Call 1974; Currier 1962, cited in Reeve 1966; Dollar 1966; Graff and Cooley 1970; Hountras and Brandt 1970). Another found, however, that students who lived at home dropped out in much larger proportion than those who lived in dormitories, apartments, fraternities, or sororities (Alfert 1966).

The mental health of college students has traditionally concerned educators. A 1955 report on the college student by the Group for the Advancement of Psychiatry was, "like most books and articles on the college student, . . . obviously attuned to the needs and problems of the residential student" (Kysar 1964, p. 472). The report recognized, however, that the number of "nonresidential" students was growing rapidly and that not enough was known about their problems to provide needed help. Lantz and McCrary (1955), believing that administrators assume that commuters are less emotionally mature than residents, tested that assumption, but their research did not substantiate it. Studying 26 variables in relation to students who lived at home with parents versus those who lived in residence halls, Drasgow (1958) reported only five significant differences. Among the differences, it was shown that residents had more worries or anxieties than commuters. On the other hand, another researcher found that commuters expressed more difficulties regarding finances, home, and family (Stark 1965). Another study concluded that commuters had "poorer mental health and curricular adjustment" and "tended to be more beset by lack of self-confidence, feelings of failure and insecurity, and excessive worry over petty disturbances" than resident students (Graff and Cooley 1970, p. 56). Other research (George 1971; Sauber 1972) indicated that commuters had different personality needs but were not necessarily less emotionally healthy or needed more help than residents.

Before Chickering's *Commuting versus Resident Students* (1974), little had been written about differences in satisfaction with college life, relationships with faculty and fellow students, and involvement in cocurricular activities. The findings of the limited research in these areas are contradictory (Baird 1969; Graff and Cooley 1970; Katz and Associates 1968), similar to those regarding academic success and mental health.

Student personnel practitioners evidenced concern for students living in rooming houses, apartments, and private homes near the campus (Mueller 1961; Shaffer 1959) without the benefit of research to document students' needs. The first comprehensive, albeit single-institution, study of students living "off campus" but not "at home" indicated that a "great majority of off-campus students have a favorable impression of the university and appear satisfied with their experience" but that "the off-campus student is, in fact, a somewhat marginal member of the university community" (Prusok 1960, p. 8). Suggested roles for personnel workers on and off campus can respond to the needs of students living in the immediate vicinity of the institution (Mueller 1961; Prusok 1960; Shaffer 1959).

The commuter institution

Although most of the early work attempted to describe the commuting experience at primarily residential institutions, the theme of the collegiate experience (or lack of it) at 100 percent commuter institutions began to be developed in the early 1960s. Primarily urban commuter institutions were characterized as "street-car colleges" where students were provincial, had little or no identity as college students, and rarely achieved degrees (Riesman and Jencks 1962, p. 105). San Francisco State College was described as "a social organization that resembled that of a factory, to which various people came for a limited number of hours each day" (p. 173). Commuter colleges, "often compared to supermarkets" (p. 115), were purely vocational in nature and did not produce alumni.

> The nature of the student body influences the character of many urban universities. "Street-car college," "subway university," and "blue-shirt institution" convey a not always accurate description of institutions located in big cities. The commuting student who is "half in and half out, half at college and half at home" is common among undergraduates (Klotsche 1966, p. 17).

Some proposed various ways to make urban commuter institutions better places to obtain a college education but used the residential model as their point of reference (Klotsche 1966; Riesman and Jencks 1962; Ward and Kurz 1969).

Descriptions of experiences as counselors of urban commuter students (Kysar 1964; Schuchman 1966) frequently have been cited as references in works that follow. Assuming that most students associated a college education with going away to college, Kysar postulated that the "commuter student has for various reasons avoided or delayed the normal developmental task of leaving home" (p. 473). Based on this premise and the fact that many of his clients were first-generation college students, Kysar hypothesized that greater numbers of "vulnerable people with a higher potential for mental disorder" attended an urban commuter university than a residential one (p. 480). Likewise, Schuchman observed that commuters who lived at home had difficulties asserting independence and finding their own identity and that these tasks were exacerbated for students of minority and lower socioeconomic backgrounds. In other urban campus studies, researchers found that commuters used services less and participated less in the social, recreational, and cultural facets of higher education than residents (Lindahl 1967; Penney and Buckles 1966).

Perpetuation of negative assumptions

Despite the inconclusive and contradictory nature of the pre-Chickering literature on commuter students, it is rife with strongly negative characterizations. Much of this work (e.g., Harrington 1974; Kronovet 1965; Kysar 1964; Schuchman 1966, 1974) was based on observation rather than on carefully designed research. Kronovet (1965), for example, stated, without sources, that commuter college freshmen were entangled in a "state of suspension between the home and the college," which "serves only to postpone or block the student's maturity and self-development" (p. 693). Schuchman (1974) defined five categories of commuter students and listed their special developmental tasks, citing only his own descriptive article from 1966 and a general reference on the effect of social class on parent-child relationships. Based on the assumption that separation from home following high school is normal, Harrington (1974) asserted that commuters experienced "a social deprivation" because they commonly had "relatively few college friends and acquaintances" (p. 10).

The impact of these ungrounded statements is compounded because they are cited repeatedly in other articles as authoritative sources of information. The first review of the literature on commuter students was published in 1972 (Harrington). It is a singularly negative portrayal that overgeneralizes the findings of limited studies and condenses them to highlight only the findings that place commuter students in an unfavorable light when compared to residents.

The Second Wave:
Major Studies, Increased Interest

Chickering (1974) and Astin (1975, 1977) dominate the second wave of literature regarding the experience of commuter students in higher education. Their work is far greater in scope and significance than previous research studies, consisting of multi-institutional studies of national samples of college students over time. Although Chickering acknowledges impending major changes in the students coming to higher education, however, his study and Astin's include only *first-time, full-time* freshmen. In addition to the focus on traditional-age students, Astin (1975) confined his research on retention to "traditional collegiate institutions" (p. 147).

Chickering's "haves" and "have nots"

Commuting versus Resident Students, the first book to focus on commuter students and their experiences, makes it clear that "the residents are the haves and the commuters, the have nots" in higher education (Chickering 1974, p. 49). When students in the national sample were aggregated for all institutions, residents came from families with more education and higher incomes, had greater high school achievements, participated in more extracurricular activities and cultural experiences before college, and had loftier educational aspirations. "Beginning college with fewer advantages than resident students, commuters as a group slip further and further behind residents . . . . And, as a consequence, college has the effect of widening the gap between the have-not students and the haves" (p. 44).

> *Whatever the institution, whatever the group, whatever the data, whatever the methods of analyses, the findings are the same. Students who live at home with their parents fall short of the kinds of learning and personal development typically desired by the institutions they attend . . . . Students who live at home, in comparison with those who live in college dormitories, are less fully involved in academic activ-*

*ities, in extracurricular activities, and in social activities
with other students. Their degree aspirations diminish and
they become less committed to a variety of long-range goals.
Their satisfaction with college decreases, and they become
less likely to return* (Chickering 1974, pp. 84–85).

Students who lived in rented off-campus housing were found
to be an extremely diverse group of students who scored dif-
ferently from both residents and commuters who lived at
home.

Clearly, in this work, the residential college experience is
the benchmark against which all others should be measured.
In it, the academic goals and developmental tasks of resident
students remain unchallenged as the "correct" ones. And the
proposed response—"thoughtful development of new arrangements [that] make residential experiences part of the
fabric of education" (p. 10)—simply is not feasible for most
commuter students.

Astin's research on college
impact and dropping out

Based on data collected annually from first-time, full-time
freshmen through the Cooperative Institutional Research Program, Astin's study (1975) found that living in a residence
hall as a freshman was associated with reduced possibilities
for dropping out. Similarly, living at home with parents neg-
atively affected persistence when compared with living on
campus. Living in a private room or apartment rather than with
parents was found to be beneficial to men and detrimental
to women. Among the most significant positive effects of living on campus versus commuting were involvement in extracurricular activities, interaction with faculty, achievement in
academic studies and leadership, career development, social
life, and satisfaction with the undergraduate experience (Astin
1977). Among the implications for educational policy makers
is the need for commuter institutions to provide opportunities
to increase students' involvement and the institution's impact.
"Is it possible to *simulate* the residential experience, at least
for those eighteen-year-olds coming directly out of high
school in pursuit of a bachelor's degree?" (Astin 1977, p. 257).

Heightened interest in commuter students

In addition to—and perhaps as a result of—the work of Chickering and Astin, the 1970s evidenced an increased interest

in commuter students and several innovative approaches to studying their college experiences. In 1972, the National Clearinghouse for Commuter Programs (NCCP) was founded at the University of Maryland at College Park as the first national organization for the purpose of sharing data and other information about commuter students and about programs and services designed to meet their needs. With the assistance of the NCCP, Educational Facilities Laboratories published the first monograph on services and facilities specifically for commuter students (1977). This publication, like the NCCP, broadly defines commuters as all students who do not live in university-owned housing and describes examples of good practice in responding to commuters' on-campus needs. In 1978, the American College Personnel Association created a permanent Commission on Commuter Programs, citing as one of its goals to conduct research to reveal "the contradictory information in regard to the stereotyped 'Have Not' images of the commuter" (Likins 1984, p. 1).

Studies focused on the heterogeneity of commuter students and on the diverse groups within the population (Educational Facilities Laboratories 1977; Foster, Sedlacek, and Hardwick 1978; Sedlacek et al. 1976; Slade and Jarmul 1975). Investigators challenged Chickering's findings regarding the detrimental effects of commuting (Davis and Caldwell 1977; Mussano 1976; Pugh and Chamberlain 1976). Researchers also began to examine *why* on-campus housing may be a primary factor in retention and the quality of the college experience, hypothesizing that such housing serves a valuable and positive function of socialization that facilitates adjustment to and satisfaction with the institution (Lacy 1978; Pantages and Creedon 1978; Welty 1976).

Nevertheless, articles continued to be published that perpetuated negative stereotypes of commuters and heavily cited the pre-Chickering sources that put forth unwarranted conclusions (Arthur 1977; Flanagan 1976). For example, using just three references (with only Chickering's work based on research), Arthur concludes that "research findings on commuting students are consistent, no matter what institution, group, data, or methodology" (p. 317).

The Third Wave: Diversity
Simultaneously with the examination of the effect of residence on the college experience of traditional college students, the

Among the implications for educational policy makers is the need for commuter institutions to provide opportunities to increase students' involvement and the institution's impact.

literature began to reflect the growing diversity of college students, among them "new students" (Cross 1971), adult learners, ethnic minorities, and students in urban and two-year college settings. The vast majority of these students are commuters.

Operationally defined as those "scoring in the lowest third among national samples on traditional tests of academic ability," "new students" are of traditional college age, mostly Caucasian, and from blue-collar families, and most often attend community colleges and other open-admissions institutions (Cross 1971, p. 13). Two-year and urban commuter institutions also enroll a disproportionately high number of minority students with low family incomes and records of low educational achievement (Richardson and Bender 1985). The necessities of economy and academic preparation force most of these students into commuting from home to college, often on a part-time basis coupled with part- or full-time employment.

During the late 1970s and 1980s, a considerable body of literature on adult students (also called returning students, stop-outs, reentry students, and older students) was published, contributing substantially to our understanding of how to facilitate adult learning (e.g., Aslanian and Brickell 1980; Brookfield 1986; Chickering and Associates 1981; Cross 1981a; Keeton and Associates 1976; Knowles and Associates 1984; Knox 1977). Research and descriptive material overwhelmingly indicate that adult learners cannot be regarded as a single, homogeneous population. Their motivations to participate in higher education are influenced by a broad range of attitudes, interests, values, expectations, and life situations (Aslanian and Brickell 1980; Hughes 1983). Like other commuting students, adult learners have been found to have multiple commitments, of which college is but one (Hughes 1983). Services designed especially for adult students are also being addressed (Heermann, Enders, and Wine 1980; Schlossberg, Lynch, and Chickering 1989).

Although hardly nontraditional students, graduate students have not been the focus of much research. A few pieces have recently appeared, describing the stresses faced by graduate students and their families, analyzing their needs for services, and suggesting some responses to those needs (Beardsley and Beardsley 1987; Driscoll and Sinderbrand 1987; McLaughlin 1985; Reisman et al. 1983).

The Fourth Wave: Commuting as the Norm and the Imperative to Respond

The fourth wave of literature regarding commuter students is characterized by a challenge to the residential bias of student services and programs and advocacy for a comprehensive response to commuter students' needs. It pushes beyond Chickering and Astin in attempting to determine the precise cause of the seemingly positive effects of living on campus.

Student services

Four categories have been proposed for sorting the variety of functions that are and should be performed to improve the quality of life for commuting students: services, programs, advocacy, and research (Jacoby and Girrell 1981). A sourcebook in the *New Directions for Student Services* series debunks myths about commuter students, proposes a comprehensive definition and demographic description of the population, suggests ways in which institutions can organize to serve commuters, and offers a developmental perspective of commuter students (Stewart 1983). In 1986, the Council for the Advancement of Standards for Student Services/Development Programs published standards and guidelines for 18 functional areas within student affairs, one of which is for programs and services for commuter students. A special issue of the *NASPA Journal* was devoted entirely to articles about commuter students and services designed for them (Jacoby and Burnett 1986b).

Examination of the direct versus indirect effects of residence

In a national survey regarding retention, most types of institutions rated commuting lowest among several variables as a characteristic likely to be found among dropouts (Beal and Noel 1980). The prevailing factors related to attrition were low academic achievement, limited educational aspirations, indecision about major/career, inadequate financial resources, economic disadvantage, and being a first-generation college student.

One multi-institution study attempted to assess the effects of residential living on four measures of outcome: educational aspirations, satisfaction with college, rate of progress through college, and intentions to persist or withdraw after two years of college (Pascarella 1984). With the influence of all other variables in his causal model held constant, Pascarella concluded that living on campus (versus commuting) had no significant, direct effects on any of the four measures of outcome. Rather, the influence of residence was at best small, indirect, and mediated through levels of involvement with faculty and fellow students. Another national study found no significant, direct influence of residence status on two measures of students' intellectual and interpersonal self-image (Pascarella 1985a). The positive influence of living on campus was again indirect in that living in residence halls had a significant, positive, direct effect on the extent of students' interactions with faculty and peers.

A study of the effects of involvement in college activities at a commuter institution found large differences in perceptions of and satisfaction with the college experience between students who participated in campus organizations and students who did not and concluded that many of the negative aspects of commuting may be mediated by encouraging participation in student activities (Abrahamowicz 1988, p. 237). Such studies, which isolate factors (other than living on campus) that enhance students' persistence and satisfaction, have strong implications for educational policy and practice.

Institution-specific research on commuters

Institutional research is the necessary foundation for improving the quality of commuter students' educational experiences. It is encouraging to note that institutions are conducting several kinds of research on their commuter students. The University of Cincinnati, for example, regularly surveys its largely commuter population on a wide variety of topics and reports findings through a research newsletter. A series of research reports derived from a longitudinal study of students at the University of Maryland at College Park analyzes students' characteristics and behaviors along several dimensions, including place of residence. The Ohio State University has published extensive descriptive data focusing on the demographics and levels of involvement of commuter students.

The Fifth Wave: The Education Reform Reports

Since 1983, numerous national commissions have issued report after report calling for substantial reform in American higher education. The reports have attracted much attention on campuses, in the chambers of government, and in the national press. Some concentrate mainly on the curriculum, while others place learning in a broader perspective.

The floodgates were opened with the report on involvement in learning (Study Group 1984), which stressed the importance of including part-time and commuting students in learning communities and cocurricular programs and activities. As for specific recommendations, however, the report stated only that "short-term but intense periods of residence" are important for "commuter, adult, and part-time students" (p. 34). A member of the study group expanded upon some of the key concepts in the 1984 report, suggesting once again that policy makers for community colleges and other commuter institutions consider funding policies that "encourage full-time attendance and support special programs (such as weekend 'residencies') designed to compensate for the relative lack of involvement that typically results from the students not living on campus" (Astin 1985, p. 176). The Education Commission of the States (1986) echoed many of the recommendations of earlier reports, admonishing institutions "to find ways to ensure greater involvement of all students in their undergraduate experience, including older students who commute to campus and have major outside responsibilities like jobs and families" (p. 15).

College: The Undergraduate Experience in America found a "deep division between commuting and residential students" (Boyer 1987, p. 219). The chapter on student residence (titled "A Home Away from Home") devotes a few pages to the importance of "bringing commuter students into the life of the college" (p. 211), observing that "the most obvious step is to make certain that someone on campus is responsible for assisting nonresidential students" and that an office should be established where commuters can go to "get help, file complaints, and learn about the special programs and services available to them" (p. 211).

A New Vitality in General Education (Task Group 1988) goes a few steps farther in suggesting ways to integrate commuter students' education into their lives. In addition to affiliating with campus residences, possibilities include classroom-based projects that link commuting students with peers and with off-campus educational and cultural experiences. Although Boyer stated that his report (which is limited to four-year institutions) will be recognized as relevant to two-year institutions as well, community college associations have released a number of reports focusing specifically on two-year institutions (Commission on the Future 1988; League for Innovation 1987; Urban Community Colleges Commission 1988).

Other than those directed expressly at community colleges, the reports calling for reform perpetuate the notion that the residential experience is the normative one and that we have to find ways for commuters to approximate that experience. It is a positive development for commuter students that the reports place the responsibility for assisting students to integrate the educational process with other aspects of their lives on the institution. The concepts of "involvement," "normal progress" toward a degree, and "identification" with the institution, however, must be reexamined and redefined when, as the reports readily point out, the vast majority of students in higher education are commuters.

The reports written under the auspices of community college organizations are particularly effective in explaining why traditional models and programs are no longer appropriate for many of today's students (Commission on the Future 1988; League for Innovation 1987; Urban Community Colleges Commission 1988).

> *What works with full-time, single, well-prepared residential students does not necessarily work with part-time students who have jobs and families and who have often experienced less academic success in their previous schooling . . . . We do not suggest a residential, four-year college model . . . . More creative ways must be found to extend the discourse, build relationships, and stir a spirit of shared goals* (Commission on the Future 1988, pp. 7, 30).

UNDERSTANDING THE STUDENT-AS-COMMUTER:
Useful Frameworks, Theories, and Models

The theories and research related to the impact of college
on students are based primarily on the experiences of traditional, residential students. As a result, many discussions of
commuter students have centered on the differences (read
"deficits") of their collegiate experiences when compared
with those of resident students. Further, many institutions
operate on the assumption that what is known about resident
students applies equally well to commuters.

Some of the theories and models developed on traditional,
residential students are transferable to work with other kinds
of students (Schlossberg, Lynch, and Chickering 1989). Multiple approaches, however, are required to address the diversity of commuter students, their varied life situations, and their
educational goals. To revise our assumptions about their experiences and development in college and to understand more
fully the nature of their interactions with the institution, the
use of several different conceptual frameworks is necessary.

Effective educational practice is generally based on theoretical knowledge (Phillips 1981). A common tool for relating concepts and theories to practice is the model. While
models cannot capture the full complexity of individuals or
relationships, they can provide useful lenses through which
both researchers and practitioners can attempt to bring a particular situation into sharper focus (Chaffee 1987).

A variety of frameworks, theories, and models is presented
here because they offer concepts useful in developing a
deeper understanding of the student-as-commuter. This rather
eclectic selection does not represent an attempt to be inclu-
sive or conclusive but rather to encourage the use of a broad
range of approaches in the quest to improve the educational
experience of commuter students.

Human Development

American higher education was founded upon the English
principle of development of the whole human being. Various
definitions of college student development—the development
of individuals enrolled in institutions of higher education—
have appeared throughout the years. One of the most useful
is the definition of college student development as:

> . . . *the application of human development theory, principles,
> and concepts in an educational setting in such a manner*

---

to identify the forms of development in students to which the institution is willing and able to commit its resources in the form of selected strategies designed intentionally to change students' knowledge, behavior, attitudes, beliefs, or values (Creamer 1984, p. 3).

Since the 1960s, theories and models of student development have flourished. As noted, many of them were created for use with students aged 18 to 22 and were based on the experiences of traditional college students, many of them white, middle-class males who attended mainly private four-year residential institutions (e.g., Chickering 1969; D. Heath 1968; R. Heath 1964; Kohlberg 1969; Perry 1970). More recently, attention has focused on the adult years. Several have presented models of adult development that are important in understanding the increasing numbers of adult learners (e.g., Gould 1972; Levinson et al. 1978; Neugarten 1968, 1975; Vaillant 1977).

Because development throughout the human life cycle is exceedingly complex and not fully understood, no theory or set of theories can provide a totally adequate description of development or how developmental change occurs (Newman and Newman 1979; Rodgers 1980). Although the theories are somewhat consistent, their comprehensiveness and complexity make them difficult to grasp and to apply. Incorporating these perspectives into our working knowledge, however, "can dramatically enrich our ability to hear more perceptively the diverse meanings underneath the motives and aspirations, words and deeds" that students bring to institutions of higher education (Schlossberg, Lynch, and Chickering 1989, p. 246).

It is important to note that theories and models of college student development in particular and of human development in general may fail to account for the influence of culture on the developmental process (Wright 1987a). Most theories presume that minority students experience developmental phenomena similarly to white students, but a few researchers have begun to recognize acculturation as a critical dimension of minority students' development that should be overlaid onto existing developmental models and theories (Wright 1987a).

In addition, human development clearly differs according to gender (Schlossberg, Lynch, and Chickering 1989; see, e.g., Belenky et al. 1986 and Gilligan 1982). Research and models addressing adult life phases have also begun to highlight differences in gender (Evans 1985b; Schlossberg, Lynch, and Chickering 1989).

An extensive examination of the relationship between the development of students in college and the practices of higher education proposes the concepts of challenge and support:

> *The institution [that] would lead an individual toward greater development must . . . present him with strong challenges, appraise accurately his ability to cope with these challenges, and offer him support when they become overwhelming* (Sanford 1966, p. 46).

Development involves challenges that bring about new, more differentiated responses. If the disequilibrium becomes too great, however, the individual will retreat; if the supports are too protective, the individual will also fail to develop (Knefelkamp, Parker, and Widick 1978). Thus, it is the balance of challenges and supports that encourages development.

In an attempt to understand human development and how educators can encourage it, three types of developmental theories are briefly presented. See Knefelkamp, Parker, and Widick 1978 and Rodgers 1980 for more complete overviews of these theoretical perspectives and the original works of the theorists.

Psychosocial theory
Psychosocial theorists, building on the work of Erikson (1963, 1968), believe that an individual develops through a sequence of stages that define the life cycle. Each developmental stage occurs with the convergence of a particular growth phase and environmental demands that pose certain developmental tasks. These tasks include the learning of attitudes, the formation of a particular facet of the self, and the learning of specific skills that must be mastered to manage that particular life phase. In general, psychosocial theorists suggest that development follows a chronological sequence; however, the timing of the stages and the mastering of the related developmental tasks are heavily influenced by the society and culture in which the individual lives.

Erikson provided the foundation for psychosocial theory by outlining eight stages of psychosocial development throughout the life span. Although Erikson's concepts lack the specificity necessary for easy translation into practice, a number of theorists have elaborated on or extended a particular aspect of Erikson's general scheme, specifically examining the effect of the social climate on shaping the identity of contemporary college students (Keniston 1971), dividing Erikson's identity-intimacy phase of young adulthood into a component set of psychological tasks or "vectors" (Chickering 1969), and identifying aspects of the college environment that affect growth along those vectors (Chickering 1969). As mentioned, several theorists have contributed to the body of work on the middle-adult stages of development (e.g., Gould 1972; Levinson et al. 1978; Neugarten 1968).

Taking the psychosocial viewpoint, educators should be aware of what age their students are, what decisions, concerns, and needs are likely be to uppermost in their minds, and what skills and attitudes they need to make those decisions and to cope with their various developmental tasks (Widick, Knefelkamp, and Parker 1980).

Cognitive development

Cognitive development theorists describe and explain development from a different vantage point, based on the work of Piaget. They understand development as a sequence of irreversible stages involving shifts in the process by which the individual perceives and reasons about the world. The majority of cognitive developmental theories describe universal sequences of stages that individuals pass through. In some cases, they specify the typical ages associated with particular phases of thinking and reasoning.

The cognitive development models of Kohlberg (1969), Loevinger (1976), and Perry (1970) are most useful in the higher education setting. Loevinger's model of ego development is the most comprehensive. She believes that each stage of development reflects a core structure that manifests itself in a specific cognitive style, a distinct intrapersonal concern, an interpersonal orientation, and an approach to moral issues. Because Loevinger's model is based on women throughout the life cycle, her work is appropriate for use for adult students (Widick, Knefelkamp, and Parker 1980). Kohlberg developed a theory of hierarchical stages of how individuals reason about moral issues, emphasizing approaches to moral education. Perry's cognitive developmental framework focuses on intellectual and ethical development, encompassing nine stages or "positions," each of which represents a qualitatively different mode of thinking about the nature of knowledge. The positions, which were developed based on a population of traditional-age college students, range from a simple, categorical view of knowledge to a complex, pluralistic view in which knowledge and truth can no longer be equated (Widick, Knefelkamp, and Parker 1980).

For cognitive development theorists, developmental change occurs when an individual who views the world in a particular way encounters an idea, problem, or dilemma that causes cognitive conflict demanding a change in mode of thinking to handle it. Sanford's concept of challenges and supports in the educational environment is particularly appropriate to the cognitive developmental perspective. Educators can assess *how* students think about important issues and *how* the environment challenges and supports their thinking (Widick, Knefelkamp, and Parker 1980).

Educators can assess how students think about important issues and how the environment challenges and supports their thinking.

Person-environment

A number of person-environment theorists have conceptualized behavior and development as functions of the person and of the actual and perceived environments. Within person-environment psychology are various theoretical perspectives. Those assuming an interactional perspective suggest that development is a result of interaction between the person and the environment (e.g., Holland 1973; Stern 1970). Other person-environment approaches (e.g., Roe 1957) focus on individual personal characteristics as the primary determinant of behavior and as the link of the person to the environment or situation. The environment perspective (e.g., Barker 1968; Moos 1976, 1979) suggests that the context or situation is the determining variable and that an individual's behavior varies from one environment to another (Walsh and Betz 1985).

No theory of the environment or of person-environment interaction is as complete or validated as the more sophisticated psychosocial and cognitive development theories (Huebner 1980). The concept of person-environment congruence that emerges from the work of several of the major theorists is useful, however. A good "fit" between persons (their needs, goals, expectations, and attitudes) and the environment (its demands, supports, and the characteristics of the persons who inhabit it) is generally hypothesized to have a positive impact on the individual. Congruence between person and environment promotes satisfaction, productivity, achievement, and growth, while incongruence creates stress and dissatisfaction and inhibits growth and performance (Huebner 1980).

The constructs of person-environment theory have recently been applied to the study of the effects of transportation, particularly commuting, on individual well-being. Several studies focus on commuters' stress related to the degree of *impedance* encountered by commuters to and from work (Novaco et al. 1979; Stokols and Novaco 1981; Stokols et al. 1978). Sources of impedance include any circumstances (e.g., traffic congestion, a late bus or subway, poor road conditions, parking difficulty) that retard or otherwise interfere with one's movement between two points. High-impedance commutes have been shown to be more stressful than low-impedance commutes, and stress on commuters has been associated with differences in mood and their performance of tasks (Novaco et al. 1979; Stokols and Novaco 1981; Stokols et al. 1978).

Campus Ecology/The Ecosystem Model
With its roots in person-environment theory, campus ecology is concerned with the interactions between students and the educational environment. Crookston's definition has been used to explain campus ecology:

It is the systematic coordination and integration of the total campus environment—the organization, the structures, the space, the functions, the people, and the relationships of each to all others and to the whole—toward growth and development as a democratic community (Banning 1980, p. 208).

Design of the ecosystem is based on this ecological perspective and provides a methodology to design and redesign the campus environment. The ecosystem model recognizes that unsatisfactory educational outcomes may be the result of a deficit in the environment rather than in the student. The campus is viewed as the client and therefore the target for intervention (Hurst 1987). The seven steps in the design process are as follows:

1. Designers, in conjunction with community members, select educational values.
2. Values are then translated into specific goals.

3. Environments are designed that contain mechanisms to reach the stated goals.
4. Environments are fitted to students.
5. Students' perceptions of the environments are measured.
6. Students' behavior resulting from environmental perceptions is monitored.
7. Data on the environmental design's successes and failures, as indicated by students' perceptions and behavior, are fed back to the designers so they can continue to learn about student-environment fit and design better environments (Banning 1980, pp. 215–16).

Intervention can begin at any step in the process. If the campus has not yet been constructed, the design process would begin at step one. Because most institutions have already established environments, values, and goals, however, the design process would more likely begin at step five with measuring students' perceptions of the campus.

The ecosystems model is based on the beliefs that every student possesses the potential for a variety of behaviors and that a given campus environment may encourage or inhibit one or more of these behaviors. The wide range of individual differences among students requires the creation of a variety of campus subenvironments. Successful campus design according to the ecosystems model must consider the diversity of students and depends upon participation of all campus members, including students, faculty, staff, administration, and governing boards (Banning and Hughes 1986).

Historical responses to the presence of commuter students on campus have placed the burden of adapting on the students themselves. Often, when commuter-specific services are provided, close scrutiny reveals that the environmental accommodation is minimal and peripheral. Campus ecology through the ecosystem design process demands institutional change to improve the fit between the student-as-commuter and the campus. For example, rather than requiring commuter students to adjust their work schedules to attend classes or to use services, the institution should adjust its patterns of scheduling courses and hours of operation (Banning and Hughes 1986).

Maslow's Hierarchy of Needs
Although Maslow's work (1982) could have been included with theories of human development, it is singled out here

because of its important implications for the student-as-commuter. Maslow's theory of priority of needs has been applied within the context of higher education to the development of student services (Eddy 1977), assessments of needs (Evans 1982), orientation programs (Moore, Peterson, and Wirag 1984), and retention interventions for low-income students (Valverde 1985).

According to Maslow, an individual cannot attend to higher-level needs when basic needs are not yet met. From lowest to highest, Maslow's hierarchical needs are (1) physiological—shelter, food, and sleep; (2) safety—protection against harm, security, consistency; (3) belongingness and love—acceptance, affection; (4) esteem—self-respect, worth, status; and (5) self-actualization—development of full potential and individuality.

This hierarchy is particularly useful in thinking about the experience of commuter students both on and off the campus. As a result of their various situations, commuter students are often preoccupied with satisfying their lower-level needs. It is essential for institutions to provide services to help meet students' basic needs for housing, transportation, food, security of person and possessions, health care, and child care. On the next level, all students need to feel a sense of belonging to and acceptance by the campus community. Before students can take full advantage of the institution to achieve self-actualization, their need for esteem must be met: The institution must demonstrate respect for the worth of each individual and accord membership in the community. A student who has not found satisfactory living or transportation arrangements is not able to concentrate fully on classwork or likely to participate in cocurricular programs. Similarly, a student who feels like a second-class citizen would most likely not seek out within the campus community the kinds of risk-taking experiences that lead to personal growth.

Mattering

The concept of mattering (Rosenberg and McCullough 1981) is related to Maslow's needs for belongingness and esteem. Mattering is defined as "the feeling that others depend on us, are interested in us, are concerned with our fate, or experience us as an ego-extension" (Rosenberg and McCullough 1981, p. 165). Rosenberg's research on adolescents indicates that those who feel that they matter to others will be less likely to commit delinquent acts. A "mattering scale" has been developed for use in determining whether policies, practices, and classroom activities in higher education are geared toward making adult students feel that they matter (Schlossberg, Lynch, and Chickering 1989).

The construct of marginality has been identified as the polar opposite of mattering (Schlossberg 1985). Commuter students have been and have felt marginal in colleges and universities since they first participated in American higher education. While feeling marginal during a period of transition into a new role or environment is to be anticipated, institutions should employ policies and practices that make all students feel that they matter to the institution, that they are central rather than marginal. The next section presents a list of questions regarding a wide range of areas, including mission, admissions, classroom environments, facilities, and funding practices, that institutions can use to assess whether commuter students truly matter.

Involvement/Talent Development/Integration
Research suggests that the more time and effort students invest in the learning process and the more intensely they engage in their own education, the greater will be their growth, achievement, and satisfaction with the college experience and their persistence toward attainment of their educational goals (Study Group 1984). Two fundamental principles of educational excellence form the basis of the Study Group's recommendations:

1. The amount of a student's learning and personal development associated with any educational program is directly proportional to the quality and quantity of the student's involvement in that program.
2. The effectiveness of any educational policy or practice is directly related to the capacity of that policy or practice to increase students' involvement in learning (p. 19).

The concept of students' involvement, incorporated into a talent development view of higher education, holds that a high-quality institution is one that "facilitates maximum growth among its students and faculty and that can document that growth through appropriate assessment procedures" (Astin 1985, p. 77). "We in higher education increasingly think of ourselves not as being in the education business but as being in the talent business—talent identification and development" (Noel 1985, p. 2). Learning and personal growth occur best in institutional environments where students' talents can be identified and developed (Noel 1985).

Many commuter students cannot become involved in the same ways that traditional-age, residential students can. More research is needed on the application of involvement theory to commuters' college experience. "Adult learners are interested in trying to connect their educational experience to the rest of their lives, and the more they can do that, the more involved they become" (Astin, cited in Richmond 1986, p. 93).

A model for understanding the process of student withdrawal is based on the degree of social and intellectual integration within the institution (Tinto 1987). This model postulates that a student's background characteristics at the time of entry influence initial commitments to the institution and to graduation. This combination of background characteristics and initial commitments in turn influences the student's academic and social integration into the institution. Students decide to leave when they are not adequately integrated into the academic and social realms of the institution, and their background characteristics influence the decision to withdraw only indirectly (Tinto 1987).

The concepts of belonging, mattering, involvement, and integration are all interrelated. They are important in assessing to what extent the institutional environment is positive for commuter students.

Transition Theory
A recent spate of professional and popular literature describes the multitude of transitions that make up adulthood, especially in the early and middle years (Aslanian and Brickell 1980; Schlossberg 1984). A transition is broadly defined as "any event or nonevent that results in change in relationships, routines, assumptions, and/or roles within the settings of self, work, family, health, and/or economics" (Schlossberg 1984, p. 43). Life transitions often serve as reasons for seeking learning (Aslanian and Brickell 1980). Transition theory "can be applied to learners young or old, male or female, minority or majority, urban or rural" (Schlossberg, Lynch, and Chickering 1989, p. 13).

A transition can be an event, such as returning to school after working for a number of years, or a nonevent, such as stopping out and reentering college over a long period of time without achieving a degree. Transitions, whether events or nonevents, change the ways individuals view themselves and alter their roles, routines, and relationships within the family, the workplace, the community, and the institution of higher education (Schlossberg, Lynch, and Chickering 1989).

A transition is not so much a matter of change as it is the individual's perception of the change (Schlossberg 1984). Thus, a transition (e.g., an 18-year-old's enrolling in a local community college while living at home) may be perceived as an event by some individuals and as a nonevent by others. The student's family may or may not view the transition the same way the student does. Students entering higher education may be simply adding a role to the others they already hold or completely redefining their roles by leaving a full-time job or placing children in day care, for example. College and university personnel should be aware that many of their students are in transition and should be prepared to assist them in adjusting to their new roles, challenges, and relationships.

Family Systems

Many commuter students live with their families. In the case of traditional-age students, it usually means parent(s) and/or siblings. Others live with their spouses and children. Grandparents or other relatives may be present in either situation. Several studies indicate that family relationships play a crucial role in the overall college experience of commuter students (Schuchman 1966; Sullivan and Sullivan 1980; Wilson, Anderson, and Fleming 1987).

Family systems theorists identify ways in which an individual's life is governed by the family (Bowen 1978). Knowledge of the workings of family units is important in understanding what are often the most influential relationships for the student-as-commuter. Eight important characteristics of the functional family help to clarify the differences between functional and dysfunctional families:

1. Family members see attractiveness and purpose in being together and support and encourage each other.

2. They respect each other's views and appreciate each other's ways of thinking and feeling.
3. They communicate openly and feel secure and positive about expressing their feelings about themselves and others.
4. Family members exhibit a high level of initiative and accomplishment rather than avoidance and procrastination.
5. Parents are close and affectionate with one another and in regard to their parenting.
6. Family members experience closeness with a high degree of individuation and support of autonomy.
7. They are open to new experiences and appreciate spontaneity without engaging in rigid and stereotypic behaviors that were more appropriate in the past.
8. Family members show a willingness to negotiate rather than to control. Clear lines of authority and responsibility exist without domination and authoritarianism (Andrews 1979, pp. 172–73).

If families are dysfunctional along one or more of these dimensions, the life of the student will be profoundly affected. One study showed that a considerable number of commuter students who were having academic or social difficulties also were experiencing some type of family crisis (Schuchman 1966).

Students whose family financial situations force them to live at home although they would prefer living on campus may feel "trapped" and that their parents are stifling their independence. Parents, on the other hand, may feel guilty and hold themselves responsible for hampering the student's ability to take full advantage of being in college. Some students may feel intense pressure to succeed in college if their parents daily reinforce their view that the student's college degree is the only means of improving the family's socioeconomic status. Other students may find parents, spouses, or children unfavorably disposed toward college because they do not see the value of higher education or because they resent the amount of time and energy the student spends in related activities (Jacoby 1983).

INSTITUTIONAL SELF-ASSESSMENT

The Need for Institution-Specific Research

A fundamental responsibility of institutions of higher education is to conduct research and evaluation to determine to what extent students' educational goals and needs are being met. This assertion is confirmed in a wide variety of literature pertinent to higher education, including works on strategic planning, organizational development, marketing, assessment of outcomes, retention, and educational reform.

A high-quality institution is one that knows about its students ... [and] has a method for gathering and disseminating this information, enabling it to make appropriate adjustments in programs or policies when the student data indicate that change or improvement is needed. In other words, quality is equated here not with physical facilities or faculty credentials but rather with a continuing process of critical self-examination that focuses on the institution's contribution to the student's intellectual and personal development (Astin, cited in Keller 1983, p. 132).

Unfortunately, institutional research in general and on commuter students in particular has been lacking. In addition to the reasons identified earlier, other factors apply directly to institution-specific research:

- Defining the population of commuter students has been problematic.
- Much of the awareness of commuter students and their needs has occurred at a time when most institutions are faced with shrinking resources.
- Low group identity and limited affiliation with the institution have caused commuters to seem "invisible" and easily overlooked (Stewart 1985, p. 165).

This sparsity of institutional research is especially inopportune because of the inconsistent and inconclusive nature of the literature on commuter students.

Even if the literature on commuter students were more definitive, however, it is not good practice to transfer conclusions about commuter students from national studies to a particular institution or from one institution to another. Although commuter students share a common core of needs and concerns, the population of commuters is extremely diverse and consists of different groups, not all of which are represented on each campus. What on one campus may be a useful and accurate statement about commuter students and their needs may be inaccurate and misleading on another.

Investigators who conduct national studies of students and the impacts of higher education agree that national research does not eliminate the need for institution-specific research and evaluation (Astin 1977; Chickering 1974; Pascarella 1982; Tinto 1987). Distinctions between commuters and residents "can be misleading if applied indiscriminately because there are significant variations among different types of institutions" (Chickering 1974, p. 49). Because higher education changes constantly, it is difficult "to be sure that effects observed in earlier long-term studies will apply to the future" (Astin 1977, p. 192). Only campus-based assessment can evaluate each institution's general approach to educating its commuter students and assess how each aspect of the institution responds to their needs.

No attempt can be made here to describe and compare various methods of collecting data. Instead, this section addresses the kinds of information that an institution must acquire about its students, its programs, facilities, services, operating assumptions, and environment, and the nature of students' interactions with the institution.

What an Institution Needs to Know about Its Commuter Students: Questions to Ask

Whether an institution has a small number of commuters or serves only commuters, basic questions must be answered if the institution is to understand who its students really are. It has already been established that commuter students are extraordinarily diverse and that the nature of the commuter population is distinct at each institution. In addition, the complexity of commuter students' life-styles and the multiple demands upon their time and energies require a wide range of information to be gathered if the nature of their relationship to higher education is to be understood.

Knowing the answers to the following basic questions will enable institutions to take the first step in dealing with the key issues related to the educational experience of the student-as-commuter.

- What percentage of the student population are commuters?
- How many students fall in the traditional age of 18 to 22 years old? How many are between 22 and 25? Between 25 and 35? Between 35 and 45? Between 45 and 55? Over 55?

Younger commuters, like residents, may identify strongly with being a college student and may desire a traditional college experience. Older students usually have different needs and expectations. Theorists who study life span and adult development confirm that adults of various ages are working on a variety of developmental tasks that may or may not be age specific. They significantly affect the student's education.

- What are the percentages of students by sex?
- How do they break down by ethnic background?

Recent literature highlights numerous and important individual differences by gender and ethnicity. Women's developmental tasks differ in some ways from men's, and women—particularly those returning to higher education—may have different educational motivations. In addition, critical distinctions exist between minority groups and the majority population as well as among various minority groups.

- How many attend full time, how many part time? When are they on campus: five days or two? Day or evening? All day or an hour at a time? Weekends only?

Full-time commuter students may want to participate actively in traditional college life. Part-time students, on the other hand, may want to get in and out as quickly as possible, placing a higher value on convenience than on campus life. Knowing when students are on campus obviously is essential in scheduling classes and activities and determining hours of availability for services and facilities.

- What is the socioeconomic status of students and their families? What is the level of education of their parents, other family members, and peers?

Research indicates that these factors are among the most powerful of the preenrollment characteristics in their influence

Adults of various ages are working on a variety of developmental tasks that may or may not be age specific.

upon the nature and success of the student's collegiate experience. At some institutions, a large proportion of commuter and/or part-time students may come from families of lower socioeconomic status where higher education has not been a priority. At others, the situation is different, and virtually no significant distinctions exist among students along these lines.

- How do students finance their education? Do they depend on their parents or spouses? Are they financially independent? Do they receive financial aid?

Some students commute and/or attend part time because their families do not have sufficient resources to send them away to college or to permit them to attend full time. Financially independent students may not be financially stable, and their college attendance may be intermittent. Financial aid is often not sufficient to meet the real needs of full-time commuter students, and aid to part-time and adult students is often limited.

- What is their employment status? Do they work full time or part time? How many hours per week? On or off campus?

Students who are fully employed in careers are likely to have different educational needs from those who work in part-time jobs to support themselves while in school. Numerous studies document that part-time work on campus contributes to retention, while working over 20 hours per week off campus has the opposite effect.

- What about family status? Do students live with their parents? What is their marital status? Do they have children? Other family responsibilities?

Negotiations with family members are required to establish priorities, commitments of time, and responsibilities. Parents, spouses, and children may be significant sources of support— or they may not understand the value of higher education and why it consumes so much of the student's time and energy. Family transitions (e.g., divorce, remarriage, birth, death) have multiple ramifications for students. Responsibilities for the care of young children and older relatives can be time-consuming and emotionally tiring.

- Where do students live? With relatives, roommates, or alone? In what type of housing? Are they responsible for rent or mortgage payments?

Students, like other people, spend more time at home than in any other place. The nature of their living arrangements determines the kinds of chores they must perform and directly affects their ability to concentrate on studying. Responsibility for rent or mortgage payments has considerable financial implications.

- How far do students live from campus?
- What are their modes of transportation?

Commuting—whether by walking, bicycling, driving, or public transportation—consumes time, energy, and financial re-sources. Commuter students often have concerns about safety and security, particularly at night. Use of public transportation involves adhering to fixed schedules, usually not optimal, and often the inconvenience of using several modes of transit. Drivers are subject to traffic jams, parking problems, car main-tenance, sharing vehicles with other family members, and the occasional need to seek alternate means of transportation. Long-distance commuters find it particularly difficult to get to campus when their cars break down. On occasion, inclem-ent weather may prevent commuters from reaching the campus.

- Do students come from the local area? From other parts of the state? From far away? From foreign countries?

Students commuting to a college near their homes and/or attending part time may feel that they are missing out on the "real" college experience of going away. They may feel that campus life is for full-time or residential students and may spend their spare time with high school friends or in com-munity activities. On the other hand, students who come from farther away are faced with more complex issues of settling and adapting to local customs than students who move into residence halls. International students must make additional and more substantial cultural adjustments.

- Why do students choose to attend this institution?

• What are their educational goals?

Students choose the institutions they attend for a wide variety of reasons. They may be bound by location, cost, or admission policy to attend a local institution. Others choose to commute because they prefer to live with family or to save money or because they believe the local institution will provide a high-quality collegiate experience. Still others may be attracted by a particular aspect of the institution, such as a specialized academic program, convenient class scheduling, or necessary services like child care. Students may or may not have clear academic and vocational goals. They may intend to complete their education in four-year, lock-step fashion or on a part-time, stop-in/stop-out basis.

• What are the relative academic abilities of commuter students? Do they need significant remedial aid?

National research offers conflicting views regarding the academic abilities of commuter students. It is absurd to assume that commuters in general or any group at a specific institution have deficient skills. It is important, however, for each institution to determine whether certain groups of students' academic abilities differ so that appropriate remedial and other support services can be provided.

Frequently, much of the data required to answer these questions already exist at the institution and are available through admissions, financial aid, registration, and institutional research offices. Standardized reports provided to the institution from such sources as the College Board, the American College Testing Program, and the Cooperative Institutional Research Program can supplement data collected by the institution. Where data do not exist, the addition of key variables to various methods of collecting data that are already in place can often provide what is needed. More and more institutions conduct separate demographic and descriptive studies of their commuter, part-time, and/or adult students. The National Clearinghouse for Commuter Programs maintains an active file of instruments and reports from these studies.

Developing an Institutional
Profile of Commuter Students
A model proposed by Rhatigan (1986) is a useful example of one method for developing an institutional profile of com-

muter students. Once some of the questions have been answered, it is possible to identify combinations of factors that characterize key groups that merit further investigation. Rhatigan suggests the creation of couplets based on variables identified as important at a specific institution (see table 2).

Any number of couplets could be added, including employed/not employed, married/single, first-time/returning, and long commute/short commute. Once the couplets of particular relevance to the institution are determined, they are combined to form a series of student profiles. As table 3 demonstrates, Rhatigan distinguishes "collegiate" from "older" combinations.

By combining the couplets, a geometric progression is developed. Table 3 includes only five (C-O, DB-OG, FT-PT, M-W, MAJ-MIN) of the eight couplets listed in table 2, resulting in 32 possible combinations (the combinations shown on the bottom half of table 3 using five variables). Using all eight

TABLE 2

VARIABLES DESCRIBING COMMUTER STUDENTS

Code	Couplets Studied
C	Collegiate (age 18–23)
O	Older (than age 23)
DB	Degree bound
OG	Other goals
FT	Full time
PT	Part time
M	Men
W	Women
MAJ	Majority race
MIN	Minority race
NR	No significant remedial problems
SR	Significant remedial problems
HA	High ability
LA	Low ability
HI	High income
LI	Low income

Source: Rhatigan 1986, p. 6.

TABLE 3

COMBINATIONS OF VARIABLES

"Collegiate" Combinations	"Older" Combinations
C-DB	O-DB
C-OG	O-OG
C-DB-FT	O-DB-FT
C-DB-PT	O-DB-PT
C-OG-FT	O-OG-FT
C-OG-PT	O-OG-PT
C-DB-FT-M	O-DB-FT-M
C-DB-PT-M	O-DB-PT-M
C-DB-FT-W	O-DB-FT-W
C-DB-PT-W	O-DB-PT-W
C-OG-FT-M	O-OG-FT-M
C-OG-PT-M	O-OG-PT-M
C-OG-FT-W	O-OG-FT-W
C-OG-PT-W	O-OG-PT-W
C-DB-FT-M-MAJ	O-DB-FT-M-MAJ
C-DB-PT-M-MAJ	O-DB-PT-M-MAJ
C-DB-FT-W-MAJ	O-DB-FT-W-MAJ
C-DB-PT-W-MAJ	O-DB-PT-W-MAJ
C-DB-FT-M-MIN	O-DB-FT-M-MIN
C-DB-PT-M-MIN	O-DB-PT-M-MIN
C-DB-FT-W-MIN	O-DB-FT-W-MIN
C-DB-PT-W-MIN	O-DB-PT-W-MIN
C-OG-FT-M-MAJ	O-OG-FT-M-MAJ
C-OG-PT-M-MAJ	O-OG-PT-M-MAJ
C-OG-FT-W-MAJ	O-OG-FT-W-MAJ
C-OG-PT-W-MAJ	O-OG-PT-W-MAJ
C-OG-FT-M-MIN	O-OG-FT-M-MIN
C-OG-PT-M-MIN	O-OG-PT-M-MIN
C-OG-FT-W-MIN	O-OG-FT-W-MIN
C-OG-PT-W-MIN	O-OG-PT-W-MIN
Etc.	Etc.

Source: Rhatigan 1986, p. 7.

of Rhatigan's couplets forms 256 potential categories of students. One can take the analysis as far as one wishes, using any set of variables that seems useful and appropriate to the institution (Rhatigan 1986). Once the profiles are developed, they can be used in assessing the various impacts of the institution on particular groups of students.

Assessing the Institutional Environment from the Perspective of the Student-as-Commuter

The institution's climate and self-image, the environment inside and outside the classroom, and the facilities, services, and programs should be thoroughly examined from the perspective of all the groups in the profile of the student body. For example, a residential college with a relatively small percentage of commuter students will want to ask itself whether commuters are simply tolerated because they help pay the bills or whether they are full partners on campus (Boyer 1987, p. 212). A large university with a high proportion of full-time, 18- to 22-year-old commuters will want to determine whether the quality of the educational experience they receive is comparable to that of residential students. And an institution that has only commuters should assess whether all students—full or part time, adult or traditional age, day or evening—are served equally well by all aspects of the institution.

Organized into categories, the following list proposes questions institutions should ask themselves in assessing whether all their students benefit equitably from the institution's offerings. Based on the profile of the student body that emerges from the data collected using the variables in the first part of this section, each institution should adapt the questions accordingly. For a comprehensive instrument specifically designed to assess institutions from the perspective of the adult learner, readers are directed to the self-study assessment compiled by the Commission on Higher Education and the Adult Learner (1984).

Mission, image, publications
All too often, an institution clings to a vision of itself that no longer reflects the composition and educational goals of many of its students. The ramifications can be far-reaching indeed when the image of an institution as traditionally collegiate (and perhaps predominantly residential)—which is incongruent with its present realities—is perpetuated in the minds

of its trustees and top officials, its mission statement, and its publications.

- Does the mission clearly reflect the present nature of the institution and its student body?
- Does the mission statement avoid terms ("traditional," "residential," "collegiate") that current and potential students could perceive as exclusionary?
- Do members of the governing board, top administrators, development officers, and public relations staff understand and describe the institution and its student body accurately?
- Are members of the institutional community proud of the institution as it is (e.g., urban, primarily commuter, serving large numbers of nontraditional students) rather than wishing it could be more "traditionally" collegiate?
- Does the institution present itself accurately in its publications? For example, do publications include photographs representing all types of students? Do they reflect a variety of life-styles?

Recruitment, admissions, articulation

Effective education depends on a sound match between students' educational goals and needs and an institution's ability to provide the appropriate opportunities, environment, and support. It is incumbent upon recruitment and admissions officers to ensure, to the best of their abilities, that this fundamental congruence exists. Because commuter students may have more limitations (often those of location and/or finances) on their choice of college, it is particularly critical to ascertain before admission that a good fit exists between what the student seeks and what the institution offers.

- Do recruiters and admissions staff clearly understand the institution's desired "mix" of students to achieve a richly diverse student body with enough commonality to support the institution's general mission and purpose?
- Do recruiters target facilities in the local area beyond high schools (e.g., community centers, primary employment sites)?
- Are preadmissions publications available at those sites and others, such as public libraries?
- Are recruiters and admissions personnel able to explain the demographics and varying life-styles of the student body?

- Do recruitment and admissions officers provide prospective commuter students with thorough and accurate information about housing, transportation, other basic commuter services offered, and campus life?
- Does the admissions office use a system of evaluation (other than high school grades and SAT scores) that reflects the life status of a wide variety of prospective students (e.g., noncognitive measures, interviews, learning and experience acquired through work and volunteer service)?
- Do policies of articulation between the institution and its feeder colleges enable a smooth transition for transfer students?

Funding and equitable fees
Often shifts in the composition of the student body occur without accompanying shifts in funding priorities. The establishment of an equitable ratio between fees and use of services is essential if all groups of the student population are to reap their fair share of benefits from the institution.

- Are commuter institutions that emphasize flexible scheduling of classes and services to meet the needs of part-time students placed at a disadvantage by state funding formulas based on full-time enrollment?
- Do services financed by student fees benefit the entire student population?
- If "traditional" services and activities are provided at no cost to users, are other services and activities (e.g., child care, family-oriented activities) offered on the same basis?
- Is revenue generated directly by certain groups of students (e.g., commuters on a largely residential campus, evening students at a primarily day institution) used to support services and programs specifically for those groups?
- Are funds for programs and other activities distributed equitably across all student groups?

Orientation and transition programs
Appreciation is growing throughout higher education of the importance of the transition into (or back into) the institution for new students, returning students, transfer students—and their families.

- Does the orientation program make all students feel equally welcome to the campus community?

- Does the program offer all students a chance to think through their educational goals and to learn about institutional opportunities and resources that can help them meet their goals?
- Do occasions exist early on for students to meet other students who are like them?
- Do all students have an equal opportunity to meet faculty and staff members and to learn about the campus "culture"?
- Are orientation activities appropriate for all students?
- Are various options for orientation available (e.g., weekday, evening, and weekend programs, individualized formats, extended orientation courses, video cassettes for home use)?

Curriculum and classroom

The single sure opportunity an institution has for significant interaction with its commuter students is in the classroom. The nature of the classroom experience is critical in engaging students in learning and in motivating them to achieve their educational goals and to become involved in other aspects of campus life.

- Do scheduling policies accommodate all students, including those who need "twilight" (4 to 6 P.M.), evening, or weekend classes as well as classes that meet once or twice a week rather than four times? Are all types of classes (e.g., upper-level, laboratory, and language) offered in alternative formats?
- Is a wide variety of courses offered during summer sessions? On a short-term intensive basis during breaks?
- Do full-time professional faculty teach evening as well as day classes?
- Does the institution encourage active modes of learning and interaction in the classroom?
- Do faculty integrate out-of-class learning and experiences into the curriculum?
- Do faculty consider commuter students' life-styles when structuring assignments (e.g., offering alternatives to group projects or projects requiring extensive time in campus libraries and computer facilities)?
- Does the institution have a program to identify students who are having difficulty and offer them assistance?

- Are different kinds of remedial programs readily available (e.g., evening and weekend hours in the learning center, computer-assisted programs, peer tutoring, materials for home use)?

Educational and career planning, academic advising, counseling

Comprehensive educational planning, advising, and counseling are important for all students. Students engaged in multiple life roles need advisers and counselors who can assist them in the ongoing process of clarifying, redefining, and pursuing their desired outcomes of the college experience. Such students' educational goals are inextricably tied to their personal and family lives and to the world of work. For some, it is critical that every course fit clearly into their educational goals and plans. In addition, commuter students often call upon advisers and counselors to serve as primary sources of information about all aspects of the institution.

- Are students offered the opportunity and encouraged to engage in comprehensive educational planning and academic advising?
- Are advisers and counselors knowledgeable about life-span development, family systems, and life transitions?
- Are advisers and counselors well informed about the institution's policies and offerings, both curricular and cocurricular (i.e., financial aid, stopping out, assessment of prior learning, internships)?
- Do advisers and counselors actively assist students in relating their education to their present work experiences and to their career aspirations?
- Are all faculty and staff members encouraged to serve as formal or informal advisers to students?
- Are placement services appropriate for students at various points in their careers rather than first-time job seekers only?
- Are peer advisers available for all students?
- Are workshops on a wide variety of personal and career topics offered at convenient times and locations?

Faculty/staff development and rewards

More and more attention is being directed toward the importance of a high-quality, caring faculty and staff who are truly concerned about students and their development. Further, all members of the campus community—from student services personnel to part-time faculty, from institutional planners to security officers, from fund raisers to food service staff—should be aware of the diversity of students and of their needs.

- Does the composition of the faculty and staff represent a wide variety of backgrounds, age groups, cultural experiences, educational institutions, and geographic origins?
- Do faculty and staff selection processes seek individuals with knowledge of and experience in working with diverse student populations?
- Are employee development programs regarding the demographics of the student body and their implications offered to all levels of faculty and staff?
- Do faculty and staff mingle with students in lounges and cafeterias frequented by commuter students?
- Do faculty and staff make personal contact with students by telephone and by maintaining an open-door policy in their offices?
- Are faculty and staff recognized and rewarded appropriately for advising students, working with student organizations, and using active modes of teaching?

Sense of community, belonging, recognition
Creating a sense of community at a commuter institution or for commuters at a mixed commuter-residential one has long challenged educators. For commuter students, feeling a part of a campus community that appreciates their individuality is an intangible yet significant determinant of persistence and of satisfaction with the college experience.

- Do campus traditions explicitly include commuter students?
- Are all students educated about the college's lore and encouraged to display the institution's symbols on notebooks, clothing, automobiles, and so on?
- Are all students encouraged to apply for academic and leadership awards? Are off-campus activities and achievements recognized as meeting criteria for awards?
- Have academic departments created areas for students and faculty to relax and talk?

- Are support groups available for students who may need them (e.g., returning women, single parents, veterans, individuals experiencing major life transitions)?

Financial aid, on-campus work, experiential learning
Financial assistance, on-campus employment, and opportunities to integrate classroom learning with experience are major factors contributing to educational success and satisfaction. They are particularly critical for commuter students, a high percentage of whom rely on work and financial aid to continue their college education.

- Do students' expense budgets for determining amounts of financial aid realistically reflect educational and living costs, including rent, food, child care, and transportation?
- Is financial aid distributed equitably to all students (e.g., adults, part-time students, students living with parents, students living independently)?
- Do financial aid officers offer educational programs about managing personal finances?
- Do administrators advocate federal and state financial aid policies and programs that would benefit the institution's students?
- Are work-study and other on-campus part-time jobs plentiful, enabling students to develop meaningful connections with the institution and with their academic programs? Are commuters informed about the advantages of working on campus?
- Are commuters encouraged to participate in internships, cooperative education, and community service?

Cocurricular activities and programs
Many students claim that their most significant gains from the college experience are obtained outside the classroom. Institutions should support cocurricular activities and programs designed to meet the needs and interests of commuters.

- Are social, cultural, educational, and intramural sports programs and activities appropriate for all students?
- Are activities and programs scheduled at a variety of times to accommodate students' varied schedules (e.g., lunchtime, early afternoon, evenings, weekends, between classes)?

Creating a sense of community . . . for commuters . . . has long challenged educators.

- Is information about activities and programs disseminated in advance so that commuters have time to rearrange their work and family schedules to attend?
- Are all types of students encouraged to participate in campus governance? In student government?
- Are "leadership ladders" available equally to all students? Is leadership training offered to all?

Outreach to significant individuals

Encouraging commuter students to become more involved in campus life often forces them to make difficult decisions about how to spend their time. Parents, spouses, children, employers, co-workers, and friends also vie for students' time. Such individuals may be important sources of support. Or, on the other hand, commuter students may feel stress at needing to explain and justify at home and at work their participation in campus activities. Institutions can develop policies and programs to support commuter students' involvement by acknowledging the roles that significant individuals play in their lives.

- Are orientation programs held for parents, spouses, and children?
- Is information about the college mailed to the homes of students' families?
- Are students' families invited to participate in campus events and activities? To use campus facilities (e.g., libraries, eateries, recreation facilities)?
- Are events held specifically for family members, such as parents' days, activities for couples, and family picnics?

Community relations

Because commuter students generally live in the communities surrounding the institution, it is to students' benefit for the college and the external communities to carry on a cooperative relationship. Many commuter students' needs are met by community agencies and services.

- Does the institution sustain active liaisons with local governments, planning commissions, housing boards, transit authorities, police departments?
- Do institutional administrators and planners keep abreast of and participate appropriately in community decision mak-

ing on behalf of commuter students regarding issues such as zoning, parking, housing, public transportation, and construction?

- Does the institution maintain positive relations with area businesses, employers, apartment complexes, and banks on behalf of its students?
- Do advisers and counselors refer students, when appropriate, to community services and agencies?
- Is information about the institution and its activities regularly published in local newspapers?
- Are members of the community invited to participate in campus activities and events?
- Does the institution sponsor activities and events in surrounding communities?

Services and facilities
All institutional services and facilities should be organized and operated to meet the needs and accommodate the schedules of all students.

Services.
- Does the institution provide assistance with students' needs for transportation (bus schedules, carpools)?
- Are information about housing and referrals provided? Are students assisted in making informed choices about housing? Is information available about utilities, schools, shopping, furniture rental, banks, tenancy, and leases?
- Are security services adequate (escorts, emergency telephones)?
- Is child care offered during day, evening, and weekend classes as well as during cocurricular programs and events? On a drop-in basis? Are referrals made to those who provide child care in the community?
- Are legal services available to students?
- Does the health service emphasize wellness, prevention, and health maintenance rather than the traditional in-patient infirmary? Is information about health and fitness distributed widely on campus?
- Are balanced meals and snacks available at times and locations convenient for all students? Are contract meal plans designed especially for commuters, both full time and part time, day and evening?

Facilities.
- Is parking adequate? Are parking lots for evening students located near classroom buildings and well lighted?
- Are adequate study areas, lounges, and lockers provided at convenient locations throughout the campus, particularly in classroom buildings?
- Are showers and emergency overnight accommodations available?
- Are recreational facilities (including lockers and showers) accessible to students at times convenient for them?
- Do commuter students have access to on-campus computer facilities for use in the early morning, between classes, evenings, and weekends?
- Is a place provided where commuter students can receive messages?
- Are "centers" available for groups of students to meet with their peers?

Scheduling and accessibility.
- Are services and facilities open at hours convenient for all students (lunchtime, evenings, weekends, early mornings)?
- Are advisers, counselors, and other administrators on flextime schedules so that they are available whenever students are on campus?
- If the institution has off-campus centers, are student services available there?
- Can students transact business (e.g., registration, bill payment) with the institution using a telephone, computer, and/or the mail?
- Are commuter students' concerns considered in the formulation and implementation of weather-related closing policies?
- Are services and facilities available during breaks, when commuter students often have more time to use them?

Information and communication
Commuter students frequently complain about the difficulty of acquiring timely and complete information about institutional policies, procedures, academic offerings, and cocurricular opportunities. Institutions should make special efforts to examine and improve their communication with commuter students, particularly with those who spend limited time on campus.

- Is a single place provided where students can go to get accurate information about the institution's policies and procedures, academic and other programs and resources, and referrals to appropriate offices or departments?
- Does a toll-free telephone information system exist for prospective and current students and their families?
- Is information disseminated in a wide variety of ways, both on and off campus: newsletters mailed to students' homes, bulletin boards, handbooks, calendars, campus and local newspapers, radio stations, cable television?
- Does the campus have a single telephone number that students can call for information about the hours of facilities and services (i.e., libraries, laboratories, tutoring)?

Analysis of Students' Interactions with the Institution

After developing a profile of the student population and examining the institution from the perspective of the student-as-commuter, the third step in institutional self-assessment is to study students' interactions with the institution. This type of research, although clearly the most complex, is the only way to determine the quality of the educational experience that students receive from the institution. Like research on commuter students in general, national studies are of little use to an institution seeking to develop policies and practices to enhance the quality of its students' educational experience.

Multiple methods of collecting data are generally necessary, some of which should be longitudinal, to determine the long-term impact of a particular factor or to assess change over time. Questionnaires, interviews, and essays may be used in combination with institutional data and other unobtrusive measures. Researchers suggest analyzing data about retention, satisfaction, involvement, choice of major, and other interactions between student and institution by key demographic variables identified in the institution's assessment of its student body (Astin 1985; Tinto 1987).

A seemingly infinite number of questions could be asked about the multidimensional interactions between students and the campus environment. The following list is intended only to suggest the kinds of questions that institutions should seek to answer for themselves:

- Do students feel that their achievements, both while enrolled and after leaving the institution, are consistent with their educational goals at the time of their entry (or return) to college?

- When and at what rate do students leave the institution? Do a higher proportion of students in some groups leave as opposed to others? Commuters versus residents? Adults versus traditional-age students? Professional versus liberal arts majors?
- What is the effect of key demographic factors and entering characteristics on grade point average? Choice of major?
- Are some groups of students more satisfied with their experience at the institution than others?
- Do some groups of students interact more with faculty and staff? What is the effect of this interaction on persistence, satisfaction, and personal development?
- Does the college experience match some students' expectations more than other students'?
- What is the effect of on- versus off-campus employment on retention, satisfaction, involvement in campus life?
- Do some groups of students participate more actively in campus activities and organizations? Why?
- Which groups of students feel that they are part of the campus community?
- Are all groups of students proportionally represented in positions of leadership, campus governance, on-campus jobs, internships, and awards?
- Do commuter students use services and facilities in proportion to the amount of fee revenue they generate?
- Do all students benefit equitably from fee-supported student activities?
- If developmental research is conducted, is it based on theoretical frameworks and models appropriate for all students?
- Are all groups of students included in any major institutional research?

Concluding Note

The process of institutional self-appraisal is nearly as important as the product in confronting negative stereotypes about students and faulty assumptions about the quality and appropriateness of the institution's programs and services. For the process to be most effective, a broad representation of members of the campus community should participate by collecting student data, evaluating their own efforts on behalf of students, and assessing the institution as a whole.

RECOMMENDATIONS FOR DEVELOPING A COMPREHENSIVE INSTITUTIONAL RESPONSE TO THE STUDENT-AS-COMMUTER

The preceding sections addressed the reasons that institutions should adopt the concept of the student-as-commuter, described useful theoretical frameworks and models, and provided a basis for institutional assessment of commuter students and the nature of their institutional experience. At this point, it is appropriate to turn to the question of how colleges and universities can and should go about enhancing the educational experience of their commuter students. In other words, if an institution really wanted to create an optimum educational environment for commuter students, what would it need to do?

Considerable change would be necessary in most institutions to create such an environment. Institutional responses to the student-as-commuter generally have been fragmented attempts to deal with immediate, specific problems rather than long-range and comprehensive. As has been shown, sheer numbers of commuter students have not been sufficient to bring about substantive changes in institutional perspectives, policies, and programs. Nor are institutions attended only by commuters necessarily providing an experience of equal quality to all their students.

Developmental Stages in an Institution's Adoption of the Concept of Student-as-Commuter

One model describes the process of institutional adaptation to adult students in three developmental stages (Ackell 1986). They range from a relatively primitive organizational stage through a more specialized type of adaptation to a final stage in which an institution has fully adapted to the point where all students are treated with equity. These developmental stages apply equally well to the process of institutional adoption of the concept of student-as-commuter. Each institution can use this model of developmental stages to determine the quality of its response to all groups within its student population (full time or part time, traditional age or older, day or evening, and so on).

Stage 1. The "laissez-faire" stage

In general, institutions in the first stage simply remove obvious barriers or artificial constraints (like requirements for admission or housing) and permit students to do the best they can within a system that works neither for nor against

---

them. Students are allowed to be as entrepreneurial and aggressive as they choose to be in dealing with the institution, but no official or organized administrative intervention is made on their behalf. The basic assumption is that variables like residence, age, and attendance status are not significant. Institutions at this stage exhibit some typical characteristics:

- Mission, publications, recruitment, admissions, and financial aid practices reflect the image of the institution's majority or "traditional" students only.
- Members of the campus community and governing board believe that the institution's "real" students are the traditional ones.
- Institutional planning does not take into account the needs of the student-as-commuter.
- No special support services or facilities are offered.
- Services financed by student fees benefit only traditional students.
- No faculty and staff development programs are available regarding the diversity of the student body and the implications of that diversity.
- No overt attempt is made to assist *all* students in obtaining financial aid, on-campus work, or internships.
- No effort exists to encourage participation by "nontraditional" students in cocurricular programs and activities.
- Some students find information about policies, procedures, and offerings difficult to obtain.
- It is unknown whether some students are consistently less satisfied with their experience and leave the institution at a higher rate than others.

Stage 2. The "separatist" stage
In this stage, certain groups of students are essentially separate from the majority of the student body (e.g., commuters on a predominantly residential campus, adults at a primarily traditional-age institution, part-time students where most attend full time). Some separate, specifically developed programs and services are provided for them, but while better than none, these programs and services have lower institutional priority and status than the traditional ones. Within this stage, it can be argued that certain student groups are subject to a subtle form of economic exploitation, as the institution expects them to function with substantially less support from

the general fund than is appropriated for programs and services for "traditional" students. This stage may include other characteristics:

- Publications, recruitment, and admissions practices acknowledge certain groups but address them as a separate population.
- Separate and different versions of programs, services, and activities are offered (e.g., orientation, workshops, advising, peer support groups).
- Minimal attempts are made to meet specific needs (e.g., housing and child care referrals, carpool lists).
- Some recognition exists that some students are "different" from the majority, usually with the assumption that they are somehow "lesser."
- Certain groups of students feel that they are not integral members of the campus community.
- Information designed for specific student groups describes their separate programs and services.
- Certain groups of students are consistently less satisfied with their experience and leave the institution at a higher rate.

Stage 3. The "equity stage"

Equity implies an "active use of the principles of justice and fairness to correct inequities in a system that de facto discriminates against one group in favor of another" (Ackell 1986, p. 3). When an institution takes steps toward treating all students fairly and providing the same quality experience for all, it has begun to evolve toward the final or equity stage of development. It is probable that no institution at the fully developed equity stage exists today in the United States, but some institutions have moved sufficiently beyond the separatist stage that some of the characteristics of a full equity institution can be discerned.

- Mission, image, publications, and institutional leadership communicate the integration of all students.
- Recruitment, admissions practices, and orientation are designed to assist all students in learning what they need to know about the institution.
- In addition to specialized services, all services, programs, and activities are organized to benefit the entire student population.

Some institutions have moved sufficiently beyond the separatist stage that some . . . characteristics of a full equity institution can be discerned.

- The concept of the student-as-commuter is used in scheduling classes and designing curricula.
- All members of the campus community share an understanding of and appreciation for the diversity of the student body.
- All students feel that they are significant members of the campus community and are recognized as such.
- Efforts are made to ensure equal access to financial aid and full participation in opportunities for on-campus employment and internships.
- Positive relationships with the community are developed and maintained on behalf of students.
- Information is disseminated in a variety of forms and is readily accessible to all students.
- Few differences exist between student groups regarding satisfaction with the college experience.

The process of development to the equity stage, where the perspective of the student-as-commuter is fully integrated into the fabric of the institution, is complex and difficult.

> *[It] involves, finally, virtually all aspects of the university's structure and function, from the board right down to the clerks and typists. It is a process [that] modifies, over time, not just part of the institution but the entire institution* (Ackell 1986, p. 5).

Developing a Plan of Action
Planning for development toward the equity stage must be established and sanctioned at the top levels of the institution's governance and administration as a systemic process and a high priority. Central leadership is of particular importance in changing an institution's priorities and in modifying and extending its activities to meet the needs and goals of all its students (Lynton and Ellman 1987).

Three categories of issues—conceptual, political, and feasibility—must be dealt with before comprehensive change can occur. Conceptual issues include the idea of the student-as-commuter, the theoretical frameworks and models presented earlier, and the need to move the institution into the equity stage of its development. Political questions often arise: Whose interests may be threatened and whose may be strengthened? Which institutional values are consistent with change and which are challenged? Issues of feasibility involve allocation and reallocation of resources, design and use of space, and staffing requirements and competencies (Schlossberg, Lynch, and Chickering 1989).

Because each institution is a distinctive combination of students, faculty, staff, mission, history, curriculum, and environment, it is impossible to provide a recipe or blueprint for change. Each institution must determine its own plan of action for moving toward the equity stage of development using the theoretical and self-assessment frameworks provided in this report. Nevertheless, it is possible to identify some key elements of a comprehensive institutional response to the student-as-commuter:

1. The institution should modify its mission statement if necessary to express a clear commitment to the quality of the educational experience of *all* its students and should have this change endorsed by its governing board.
2. The president, vice presidents, deans, and all other top administrators should frequently and consistently articulate the institution's commitment to the student-as-commuter when dealing with faculty, staff, students, the governing board, alumni, community members, and others.
3. The institution should engage in comprehensive, regular collection of data about its students and their experiences with the institution.
4. Regular processes of evaluation should be put in place to assess whether the institution's programs, services, facilities, and resources address the needs of all students equitably.
5. Steps should be taken to identify and rectify stereotypes or inaccurate assumptions held by members of the campus community about commuter students and to ensure that commuter students are treated as full members of the campus community.
6. Long- and short-range administrative decisions regarding resources, policies, and practices should consistently include the perspective of the student-as-commuter.
7. In recognition that students' experiences in one segment of the institution profoundly affect their experiences in other segments and their perception of their educational experience as a whole, quality practices should be *consistent* throughout the institution.

8. Classroom experiences and interactions with faculty should be recognized as playing the major role in determining the overall quality of commuter students' education.
9. Curricular and cocurricular offerings should complement one another, and considerable energy should be directed to ensure that students understand the interrelationship of the curriculum and the cocurriculum.
10. Faculty and staff at all levels should be encouraged to learn more about the theoretical frameworks and models that lead to a fuller understanding of the student-as-commuter.
11. Top leadership should actively encourage the various campus units to work together to implement change on behalf of the student-as-commuter.
12. Technology should be used to the fullest extent possible to improve the institution's ability to communicate with its students and to streamline its administrative processes.
13. Executive officers and governing board members should actively work toward ensuring that commuter students and commuter institutions are treated fairly in federal, state, and local decision making (e.g., student financial aid, institutional funding formulas).

As the students pursuing higher education continue to become more diverse and as diverse students attend a wider range of institutions, an understanding of the student-as-commuter and of the nature of commuter students' relationships to higher education is required to bring about necessary changes. In the current climate, institutions of higher education seek "excellence" and are held accountable for translating excellence into educational outcomes for all students. Institutional change requires substantial effort and commitment, but failure to respond effectively and comprehensively to the needs and educational goals of the student-as-commuter will make excellence impossible to achieve.

REFERENCES

The Educational Resources Information Center (ERIC) Clearinghouse on Higher Education abstracts and indexes the current literature on higher education for inclusion in ERIC's data base and announcement in ERIC's monthly bibliographic journal, *Resources in Education* (RIE). Most of these publications are available through the ERIC Document Reproduction Service (EDRS). For publications cited in this bibliography that are available from EDRS, ordering number and price code are included. Readers who wish to order a publication should write to the ERIC Document Reproduction Service, 3900 Wheeler Avenue, Alexandria, Virginia 22304. (Phone orders with VISA or MasterCard are taken at 800/227-ERIC or 703/823-0500.) When ordering, please specify the document (ED) number. Documents are available as noted in microfiche (MF) and paper copy (PC). If you have the price code ready when you call EDRS, an exact price can be quoted. The last page of the latest issue of *Resources in Education* also has the current cost, listed by code.

Abrahamowicz, Daniel. 1988. "College Involvement, Perceptions, and Satisfaction: A Study of Membership in Student Organizations." *Journal of College Student Development* 29: 223–38.

Ackell, Edmund F. 1986. "Adapting the University to Adult Students: A Developmental Perspective." In *Improving Institutional Services to Adult Learners,* edited by William H. Warren. Washington, D.C.: American Council on Education.

Adelman, Clifford. January/February 1988. "Transfer Rates and the Going Mythologies: A Look at Community College Patterns." *Change* 20: 38–41.

Adolphus, Stephen H., ed. 1984. *Equality Postponed.* New York: College Entrance Examination Board. ED 275 222. 177 pp. MF–01; PC not available EDRS.

Alfert, Elizabeth. 1966. "Housing Selection, Need Satisfaction, and Drop-out from College." *Psychological Reports* 19: 183–86.

Altman, Irwin, Joachim F. Wohlwill, and Peter B. Everett, eds. 1981. *Transportation and Behavior.* New York: Plenum Press.

American Council on Education. 1987. *1986–87 Fact Book on Higher Education.* Washington, D.C.: Author.

Andersen, Charles J., and Frank J. Atelsek. 1982. *An Assessment of College Housing and Physical Plant.* Higher Education Panel Report No. 55. Washington, D.C.: American Council on Education.

Andrews, Ernie E. 1979. "Understanding and Working with Family Units." In *Helping Clients with Special Concerns,* edited by Sheldon Eisenberg and Lewis E. Patterson. Boston: Houghton Mifflin.

Apps, Jerold W. 1981. *The Adult Learner on Campus: A Guide for Instructors and Administrators.* Chicago: Follett.

———. 1985. *Improving Practice in Continuing Education.* San Francisco: Jossey-Bass.

Apps, Jerold W., Robert D. Boyd, and Associates. 1980. *Redefining the Discipline of Adult Education.* San Francisco: Jossey-Bass.

Arbeiter, Solomon, Carol B. Aslanian, Frances A. Schmerbeck, and Henry M. Brickell. 1978. *Forty Million Americans in Career Transition: The Need for Information.* New York: College Entrance Examination Board.

Arbuckle, Dugald S. 1953. *Student Personnel Services in Higher Education.* New York: McGraw-Hill.

Arthur, Sara. 1977. "Designing Ways to Serve the Commuting Student." *Liberal Education* 63: 316–21.

Aslanian, Carol B., and Henry M. Brickell. 1980. *Americans in Transition: Life Changes as Reason for Adult Learning.* New York: College Entrance Examination Board.

Astin, Alexander W. Summer 1973. "The Impact of Dormitory Living on Students." *Educational Record* 54: 204–10.

———. 1975. *Preventing Students from Dropping Out.* San Francisco: Jossey-Bass.

———. 1977. *Four Critical Years.* San Francisco: Jossey-Bass.

———. 1982. *Minorities in American Higher Education.* San Francisco: Jossey-Bass.

———. Winter 1984. "A Look at Pluralism in the Contemporary Student Population." *NASPA Journal* 21: 2–11.

———. 1985. *Achieving Educational Excellence.* San Francisco: Jossey-Bass.

Astin, Alexander W., Kenneth C. Green, and William S. Korn. 1987. *The American Freshman: Twenty-Year Trends.* Los Angeles: Univ. of California, Cooperative Institutional Research Program. ED 279 279. 225 pp. MF–01; PC not available EDRS.

Astin, Helen Stavridou. 1976. "Continuing Education and the Development of Adult Women." *Counseling Psychologist* 6(1): 55–60.

Avakian, Nancy A., Arthur C. MacKinney, and Glenn R. Allen. 1982. "Race and Sex Differences in Student Retention at an Urban University." *College and University:* 160–65.

Baird, Leonard L. 1969. "The Effects of College Residence Groups on Students' Self-Concepts, Goals, and Achievements." *Personnel and Guidance Journal* 47: 1015–21.

Baker, S.R. 1966. "The Relationship between Student Residence and Perception of Environmental Press." *Journal of College Student Personnel* 7: 222–32.

Banning, James H. 1980. "The Campus Ecology Manager Role." In *Student Services: A Handbook for the Profession,* edited by Ursula Delworth, Gary Hanson, and Associates. San Francisco: Jossey-Bass.

Banning, James H., and Blanche M. Hughes. Summer 1986. "Designing the Campus Environment with Commuter Students." *NASPA Journal* 24: 17–24.

Barker, R.G. 1968. *Ecological Psychology: Concepts and Methods for*

Studying the Environment of Human Behavior. Stanford, Calif.:
Stanford Univ. Press.

Barr, Margaret J., et al. February 1988. "Toward an Expansion of Theory and Application in Human Development." A proposal to the
executive council of ACPA from the senior scholars of ACPA.

Beal, Phillip E., and Lee Noel. 1980. *What Works in Student Retention: A Report.* Iowa City: American College Testing Program/
National Center for Higher Education Management Systems.

Beardsley, Katherine Pedro, and Robert S. Beardsley. December 1987.
"The Forgotten Commuter: The Graduate Student." *The Commuter*
13: 5–7.

Beder, Harold W., and Gordon G. Darkenwald. 1982. "Differences
between Teaching Adults and Preadults: Some Propositions and
Findings." *Adult Education* 32: 142–55.

Belenky, Mary Field, Blythe McVicker Clinchy, Nancy Rule Gold-
berger, and Jill Mattuck Tarule. 1986. *Women's Ways of Knowing.*
New York: Basic Books.

Bender, Louis W., and Richard C. Richardson, Jr. 1987. "Urban Com-
munity College Students: An Autobiographic Profile." Tallahassee:
Florida State Univ., College of Education, Center for State and
Regional Leadership. ED 278 434. 61 pp. MF–01; PC–03.

Billson, Janet Mancini, and Margaret Brooks Terry. 1982. "In Search
of the Silken Purse: Factors in Attrition among First-Generation
Students." *College and University:* 57–75.

Bishop, John B., and Grant S. Snyder. 1976. "Commuters and Residents: Pressures, Helps, and Psychological Services." *Journal of
College Student Personnel* 17: 232–35.

Bok, Derek. 1986. *Higher Learning.* Cambridge, Mass.: Harvard Univ.
Press.

Boone, Edgar J., Ronald W. Shearon, Estelle E. White, and Associates.
1980. *Serving Personal and Community Needs through Adult Education.* San Francisco: Jossey-Bass.

Bowen, Howard R. 1977. *Investment in Learning.* San Francisco:
Jossey-Bass.

———. 1980. "A Nation of Educated People." *Liberal Education* 66:
132–40.

Bowen, Murray. 1978. *Family Therapy in Clinical Practice.* New York:
Jason Aronson.

Bown, Oliver H., and Herbert G. Richek. 1968. "The Mental Health
of Commuter College Students: A Partial Test of Kysar's Hypothe-
sis." *Mental Hygiene* 52: 354–59.

Boyer, Ernest L. 1987. *College: The Undergraduate Experience in
America.* New York: Harper & Row.

Brodzinski, Frederick R. Spring 1984. "The Role of the Chief Student
Affairs Officer in Serving Adult Learners." *NASPA Journal* 21:
48–50.

Brookfield, Stephen D. 1986. *Understanding and Facilitating Adult Learning.* San Francisco: Jossey-Bass.

Burnett, Dana. May 1982. "Traditional-Aged Commuter Students: A Review of the Literature." *NASPA Forum* 2: 6–7.

Call, R.W. 1974. *A Comparison of Resident Students' Quality Point Averages with Those of Commuting Students.* Washington, D.C.: U.S. Dept. of Health, Education, and Welfare, Office of Education.

Center for Education Statistics. April 1988. *Trends in Minority Enrollment in Higher Education: Fall 1976–Fall 1986.* Washington, D.C.: U.S. Dept. of Education. ED 297 662. 28 pp. MF–01; PC–02.

Chaffee, Ellen Earle. 1987. "Organizational Concepts Underlying Governance and Administration." In *Key Resources on Higher Education, Governance, Management, and Leadership,* edited by Marvin W. Peterson. San Francisco: Jossey-Bass.

Chickering, Arthur W. 1969. *Education and Identity.* San Francisco: Jossey-Bass.

———. 1972. "Undergraduate Academic Experience." *Journal of Educational Psychology* 63: 134–43.

———. 1974. *Commuting versus Resident Students.* San Francisco: Jossey-Bass.

———. 1984. "Education and Identity Revisited." *Journal of College Student Personnel* 25: 392–99.

Chickering, Arthur W., and Associates. 1981. *The Modern American College.* San Francisco: Jossey-Bass.

Clodfelter, Irene, Susan Furr, and Dale Wachowiak. Summer 1984. "Student Living Arrangements and Their Perceived Impact on Academic Performance." *Journal of College and University Student Housing* 14: 18–21.

Cohen, Arthur M., and Florence B. Brawer. 1982. *The American Community College.* San Francisco: Jossey-Bass.

Cohen, Arthur M., James C. Palmer, and K. Diane Zwemer. 1986. *Key Resources on Community Colleges.* San Francisco: Jossey-Bass.

College Entrance Examination Board. 1988. *Annual Survey of Colleges, 1987–88: Summary Statistics.* New York: Author.

Commission on the Future of Community Colleges. 1988. *Building Communities: A Vision for a New Century.* Washington, D.C.: American Association of Community and Junior Colleges. ED 293 578. 58 pp. MF–01; PC not available EDRS.

Commission on Higher Education and the Adult Learner. 1984. *Postsecondary Education Institutions and the Adult Learner: A Self-Study Assessment and Planning Guide.* Washington, D.C.: American Council on Education.

Commission on National Challenges in Higher Education. 1988. *Memorandum to the 41st President of the United States.* Washington, D.C.: American Council on Education.

Commuter Student Affairs Office. April 1988. "Fifty Plus Portraits:

Research Highlights of Ohio State University's Majority Student Population." Columbus: Ohio State Univ.

Council for the Advancement of Standards. 1986. *CAS Standards and Guidelines for Student Services/Development Programs.* Available from CAS Secretary, Office of the Vice President for Student Affairs, Univ. of Maryland at College Park.

Creamer, Don G. 1984. "Student Development in Urban Commuter Colleges." ED 245 634. 32 pp. MF–01; PC–02.

―――, ed. 1980. *Student Development in Higher Education: Theories, Practices, and Future Directions.* ACPA Media Publication No. 27. Alexandria, Va.: American College Personnel Association.

Creamer, Don G., and Charles R. Dassance, eds. 1986. *Opportunities for Student Development in Two-Year Colleges.* NASPA Monograph No. 6. Portland, Ore.: National Association of Student Personnel Administrators. ED 277 918. 95 pp. MF–01; PC–04.

Cross, K. Patricia. 1971. *Beyond the Open Door: New Students to Higher Education.* San Francisco: Jossey-Bass.

―――. 1981a. *Adults as Learners.* San Francisco: Jossey-Bass.

―――. 1981b. "Community Colleges on the Plateau." *Journal of Higher Education* 52: 113–23.

Daloz, Laurent A. 1986. *Effective Teaching and Mentoring.* San Francisco: Jossey-Bass.

Davis, Joe L., and Steve Caldwell. 1977. "An Intercampus Comparison of Commuter and Residential Student Attitudes." *Journal of College Student Personnel* 18: 287–90.

Deegan, William L., Dale Tillery, and Associates. 1985. *Renewing the American Community College.* San Francisco: Jossey-Bass.

Delworth, Ursula, Gary Hanson, and Associates. 1980. *Student Services: A Handbook for the Profession.* San Francisco: Jossey-Bass.

Desler, Mary K. 1987. "A Test of Tinto's Theoretical Model of College Student Persistence among Transfer Students at an Urban University." Paper presented at an ACPA/NASPA national convention, March, Chicago, Illinois.

Dollar, Robert J. 1966. "Student Characteristics and Choice of Housing." *Journal of College Student Personnel* 7: 147–50.

Donavan, Richard A., and Barbara Schaier-Peleg. January/February 1988. "Making Transfer Work: A Practical Blueprint for Colleges." *Change* 20: 33–37.

Drasgow, James. 1958. "Differences between College Students." *Journal of Higher Education* 29: 216–18.

Driscoll, Nancy S., and Allyn Sinderbrand. December 1987. "Student Services for Graduate Business Students." *The Commuter* 13: 1–3.

Dubin, Samuel S., and Morris Okun. 1973. "Implications of Learning Theories for Adult Education." *Adult Education* 24: 3–19.

Eddy, John. 1977. *College Student Personnel Development, Administration, and Counseling.* Washington, D.C.: University Press of

America.

Educational Facilities Laboratories. 1977. *The Neglected Majority: Facilities for Commuter Students.* New York: Author.

Education Commission of the States. 1986. *Transforming the State Role in Undergraduate Education.* Denver: Working Party on Effective State Action to Improve Undergraduate Education. ED 275 219. 45 pp. MF–01; PC not available EDRS.

El-Khawas, Elaine. August 1987. *Campus Trends, 1987.* Higher Education Panel Report No. 75. Washington, D.C.: American Council on Education. ED 286 402. 52 pp. MF–01; PC–03.

Ender, Steven C., Thomas J. Grites, Theodore K. Miller, Roger B. Winston, and Associates. 1984. *Developmental Academic Advising: Addressing Students' Educational, Career, and Personal Needs.* San Francisco: Jossey-Bass.

Erikson, Erik. 1963. *Childhood and Society.* 2d ed. New York: Norton.

———. 1968. *Identity, Youth, and Crisis.* New York: Norton.

Evans, Nancy J. Spring 1982. "Using Developmental Theory in Needs Assessment." *Journal of NAWDAC* 45: 34–39.

———. 1985a. "Needs Assessment Methodology: A Comparison of Results." *Journal of College Student Personnel* 26: 107–14.

———, ed. 1985b. *Facilitating the Development of Women.* New Directions for Student Services No. 29. San Francisco: Jossey-Bass.

Evans, Thomas D. January 1970. "Parent and Student Perceptions of a Commuter Campus." *NASPA Journal* 7: 164–69.

Feldman, Kenneth A., and Theodore M. Newcomb. 1969. *The Impact of College on Students.* San Francisco: Jossey-Bass.

Flanagan, Dan. Spring 1976. "The Commuter Student in Higher Education: A Synthesis of the Literature." *NASPA Journal* 13: 35–41.

Fleming, Jacqueline. 1984. *Blacks in College.* San Francisco: Jossey-Bass.

Flynn, R. Thomas. Summer 1986. "The Emerging Role for Community College Student Affairs Personnel." *NASPA Journal* 24: 36–42.

Foster, Margaret E., William E. Sedlacek, and Mark W. Hardwick. Fall 1978. "A Comparison of Potential Dependent Commuters, Independent Commuters, and Resident Students." *Journal of NAWDAC* 42: 36–42.

Foster, Margaret E., William E. Sedlacek, Mark W. Hardwick, and Anne E. Silver. 1977. "Student Affairs Staff Attitudes toward Students Living Off Campus." *Journal of College Student Personnel* 18: 291–97.

Garland, Peter H. 1985. *Serving More Than Students: A Critical Need for College Student Personnel Services.* ASHE-ERIC Higher Education Report No. 7. Washington, D.C.: Association for the Study of Higher Education. ED 267 678. 156 pp. MF–01; PC–07.

Garni, Kenneth F. 1974. "Urban Commuter Students: Counseling for Survival." *Journal of College Student Personnel* 15: 465–69.

George, Rickey L. 1971. "Resident or Commuter: A Study of Personality Differences." *Journal of College Student Personnel* 12: 216–19.

Gilligan, Carol. 1982. *In a Different Voice.* Cambridge, Mass.: Harvard Univ. Press.

Glass, J. Conrad, Jr., and Hubert H. Hodgin. 1977. "Commuting Students and Cocurricular Activities." *Personnel and Guidance Journal* 55: 253–56.

Glass, J. Conrad, and Anita R. Rose. Fall 1987. "Reentry Women: A Growing and Unique College Population." *NASPA Journal* 25: 110–19.

Goldberg, Arthur. July 1973. "Reflections of a Two-Year College Dean." *NASPA Journal* 11: 39–42.

Gould, R. 1972. "The Phases of Adult Life." *American Journal of Psychiatry* 5: 521–31.

Graff, Robert W., and Gary R. Cooley. 1970. "Adjustment of Commuter and Resident Students." *Journal of College Student Personnel* 11: 54–57.

Grant, Gerald, et al. 1979. *On Competence.* San Francisco: Jossey-Bass.

Grobman, Arnold B. 1980. "The Missions of Urban Institutions." *Liberal Education* 66: 200–207.

Hall, William M., and Warren J. Valine. 1977. "The Relationship between Self-Concept and Marital Adjustment for Commuter College Students." *Journal of College Student Personnel* 18: 298–300.

Hardy, Clifford A., and John A. Williamson. 1974. "Satisfaction with College: Commuter vs. Resident Students." *Improving College and University Teaching* 22: 47–48.

Hareven, Tamara K., and Kathleen J. Adams, eds. 1982. *Aging and Life Course Transitions: An Interdisciplinary Perspective.* New York: Guilford Press.

Harrington, Thomas F. 1972. "The Literature on the Commuter Student." *Journal of College Student Personnel* 13: 546–50.

———. 1974. *Student Personnel Work in Urban Colleges.* New York: Intext Educational Publishers.

Hatala, Robert J. 1977. "Some Thoughts on Reaching the Commuting Student." *Liberal Education* 63: 309–15.

Heath, Douglas H. 1968. *Growing Up in College.* San Francisco: Jossey-Bass.

Heath, Roy. 1964. *The Reasonable Adventurer.* Pittsburgh: Univ. of Pittsburgh Press.

Heerman, Barry, Cheryl Coppeck Enders, and Elizabeth Wine, eds. 1980. *Serving Lifelong Learners.* New Directions for Community Colleges No. 8. San Francisco: Jossey-Bass.

Heida, Debbie. Summer 1986. "Greek Systems on Predominantly Commuter Campuses." *NASPA Journal* 24: 48–50.

Henton, June, Leanne Lamke, Cassie Murphy, and Lynda Haynes. 1980. "Crisis Reactions of College Freshmen as a Function of Family Support Systems." *Personnel and Guidance Journal* 60: 508–11.

Hodgkinson, Harold L. 1985. *All One System.* Washington, D.C.: Institute for Educational Leadership. ED 261 101. 22 pp. MF–01; PC not available EDRS.

Holland, John L. 1973. *Making Vocational Choices: A Theory of Careers.* Englewood Cliffs, N.J.: Prentice-Hall.

Hooper, J.O., and G.B. March. 1980. "The Female Single Parent in the University." *Journal of College Student Personnel* 21: 141–46.

Horowitz, Helen L. 1987. *Campus Life.* Chicago: Univ. of Chicago Press.

Hountras, Peter T., and Kenneth R. Brandt. 1970. "Relation of Student Residence to Academic Performance in College." *Journal of Educational Research* 63: 351–54.

Huebner, Lois A. 1980. "Interaction of Student and Campus." In *Student Services: A Handbook for the Profession,* edited by Ursula Delworth, Gary R. Hanson, and Associates. San Francisco: Jossey-Bass.

———, ed. 1979. *Redesigning Campus Environments.* New Directions for Student Services No. 8. San Francisco: Jossey-Bass.

Hughes, Rees. Winter 1983. "The Nontraditional Student in Higher Education: A Synthesis of the Literature." *NASPA Journal* 20: 51–64.

Hurst, James C. Summer 1987. "Student Development and Campus Ecology: A Rapprochement." *NASPA Journal* 25: 4–17.

Jacoby, Barbara. 1983. "Parents of Dependent Commuters: A Neglected Resource." In *Commuter Students: Enhancing Their Educational Experiences,* edited by Sylvia S. Stewart. New Directions for Student Services No. 24. San Francisco: Jossey-Bass.

———. Summer 1986. "Sources of Support and Information for Professionals Who Work with Commuter Students." *NASPA Journal* 24: 51–54.

———. 1987. "Partnerships between Preparation and Practice: Working with Commuting Students." Paper presented at an ACPA/NASPA national convention, March, Chicago, Illinois.

Jacoby, Barbara, and Dana Burnett. Summer 1986a. "Introduction to the Commuter Issue." *NASPA Journal* 24: 2–3.

———, eds. Summer 1986b. Special Issue on Commuter Students. *NASPA Journal* 24.

Jacoby, Barbara, and Kristin W. Girrell. Winter 1981. "A Model for Improving Services and Programs for Commuter Students." *NASPA Journal* 18: 38–41.

Jacoby, Barbara, and William L. Thomas, Jr. Summer 1986. "Introduction to the CAS Standards and Guidelines for Commuter Student Programs and Services." *NASPA Journal* 24: 55–57.

Johnson, Deborah Hazel, Karen Weiss Wallace, and William E. Sedlacek. Spring 1979. "A Comparison of the Needs of Returning and Traditional Students by Sex." *Journal of NAWDAC* 42: 14–18.

Johnson, Dixon C., Robert L. Bowlin, and Robert A. Ellis. 1968. "Parental Reaction toward Off-Campus Living for Freshmen." *Journal of College Student Personnel* 9: 161–64.

Jones, John D., and Jeffrey Damron. 1987. *Student Affairs Programs at Universities in Urban Settings.* Washington, D.C.: National Association of State Universities and Land-Grant Colleges.

Kanter, Rosabeth M. 1983. *The Change Masters.* New York: Simon & Schuster.

Kasworm, Carol E. 1980a. "The Older Student as an Undergraduate." *Adult Education* 31: 30–47.

———. 1980b. "Student Services for the Older Undergraduate Student." *Journal of College Student Personnel* 21: 163–69.

Katz, Joseph, ed. 1985. *Teaching as though Students Mattered.* New Directions for Teaching and Learning No. 21. San Francisco: Jossey-Bass.

Katz, Joseph, and Associates. 1968. *No Time for Youth.* San Francisco: Jossey-Bass.

Keeton, Morris T., and Associates. 1976. *Experiential Learning.* San Francisco: Jossey-Bass.

Keller, George. 1983. *Academic Strategy: The Management Revolution in American Higher Education.* Baltimore: Johns Hopkins Press.

Keniston, Kenneth. 1971. *Youth and Dissent.* New York: Harcourt Brace Jovanovich.

Klotsche, J. Martin. 1966. *The Urban University.* New York: Harper & Row.

Knefelkamp, Lee, Clyde A. Parker, and Carol Widick, eds. 1978. *Applying New Developmental Findings.* New Directions for Student Services No. 4. San Francisco: Jossey-Bass.

Knefelkamp, L. Lee, and Sylvia Stewart. 1983. "Toward a New Conceptualization of Commuter Students: The Developmental Perspective." In *Commuter Students: Enhancing Their Educational Experiences,* edited by Sylvia S. Stewart. New Directions for Student Services No. 24. San Francisco: Jossey-Bass.

Knowles, Malcom S., and Associates. 1984. *Andragogy in Action.* San Francisco: Jossey-Bass.

Knox, Alan B. 1977. *Adult Development and Learning.* San Francisco: Jossey-Bass.

———. 1986. *Helping Adults Learn.* San Francisco: Jossey-Bass.

Knox, Alan B., and Associates. 1980. *Developing, Administering, and Evaluating Adult Education.* San Francisco: Jossey-Bass.

Kohlberg, Lawrence. 1969. *Stage and Sequence: The Cognitive-Developmental Approach to Socialization Theory and Research.* New York: Rand McNally.

Kronovet, Esther. 1965. "Freshman Reactions to Parents' Seminars on a Commuter Campus." *Personnel and Guidance Journal* 71: 692–95.

Kuh, George D., and Frank P. Ardaiolo. 1979. "A Comparison of the Personality Characteristics of Adult Learners and Traditional Age Freshmen." *Journal of College Student Personnel* 20: 329–35.

Kuh, George D., and J. Thomas Sturgis. 1980. "Looking at the University through Different Sets of Lenses: Adult Learners' and Traditional Age Students' Perceptions of the University Environments." *Journal of College Student Personnel* 21: 483–90.

Kysar, John E. 1964. "Mental Health in an Urban Commuter University." *Archives of General Psychiatry* 11: 472–83.

Lackey, P.N. 1977. "Commuter Students' Interaction in Two Types of Class Situations." *College Student Journal* 11: 153–55.

Lacy, William B. 1978. "Interpersonal Relationships as Mediators of Structural Effects: College Student Socialization in a Traditional and an Experimental University Environment." *Sociology of Education* 51: 201–11.

Lantz, Herman R., and J.S. McCrary. 1955. "An Analysis of Parent-Student Relationships of University Student Commuters and Non-commuters." *Journal of Counseling Psychology* 2: 43–46.

League for Innovation in the Community College. 1987. *Assuring Student Success in the Community College: The Role of Student Development Professionals.* Laguna Hills, Calif.: Author.

Leinemann, William H., and Anne E. Smith. 1974. "College in the City: Commuters and Commuting Houses." *Improving College and University Teaching* 22: 55–58.

Lenz, Elinor. 1980. *Creating and Marketing in Continuing Education.* New York: McGraw-Hill.

Levine, Arthur. 1980. *When Dreams and Heroes Died: A Portrait of Today's College Student.* San Francisco: Jossey-Bass.

Levinson, Daniel J., et al. 1978. *The Seasons of a Man's Life.* New York: Knopf.

Levitz, Randi, Lee Noel, Diana Saluri, and Associates. 1985. *Increasing Student Retention.* San Francisco: Jossey-Bass.

Likins, Jeanne M. 1984. "The Creation of ACPA's Commission XVII (Commuter Programs): A Brief Historical Overview." Mimeographed.

———. Summer 1986. "Developing the Commuter Perspective: The Art of Advocacy." *NASPA Journal* 24: 11–16.

———. 1988. "Knowing Our Students: A Descriptive Profile of Commuter Students at a Large, Public, Midwestern University." Unpublished manuscript. Columbus: Ohio State Univ.

Lindahl, Charles. 1967. "Impact of Living Arrangements on Student Environmental Perceptions." *Journal of College Student Personnel* 8: 10–15.

Lindquist, Jack. 1981. "Professional Development." In *The Modern American College,* edited by Arthur W. Chickering and Associates. San Francisco: Jossey-Bass.

Liu, Richard, and Loren Jung. 1980. "The Commuter Student and Student Satisfaction." *Research in Higher Education* 12: 215–26.

Loevinger, Jane. 1976. *Ego Development.* San Francisco: Jossey-Bass.

Long, Huey B., Roger Hiemstra, and Associates. 1980. *Changing Approaches to Studying Adult Education.* San Francisco: Jossey-Bass.

Lowenthal, Marjorie Fiske, Majda Thurner, David Chiraboga, and Associates. 1975. *Four Stages of Life.* San Francisco: Jossey-Bass.

Lundgren, David C., and Marcy R. Schwab. 1979. "The Impact of College on Students: Residential Context, Relations with Parents and Peers, and Self-Esteem." *Youth and Society* 10: 227–36.

Lynton, Ernest A., and Sandra E. Ellman. 1987. *New Priorities for the University.* San Francisco: Jossey-Bass.

McAleenan, Andrea C., and George D. Kuh. 1986. "The Context for Student Affairs Work in Small Colleges." In *Student Affairs Work in Small Colleges,* edited by George D. Kuh and Andrea C. McAleenan. NASPA Monograph No. 5. Columbus, Ohio: National Association of Student Personnel Administrators.

McGraw, Linda K. 1982. "A Selective Review of Programs and Counseling Interventions for the Reentry Woman." *Personnel and Guidance Journal* 62: 469–72.

McLaughlin, Mike C. 1985. "Graduate School and Families: Issues for Academic Departments and University Mental Health Professionals." *Journal of College Student Personnel* 26: 488–91.

Maslow, Abraham H. 1982. *Toward a Psychology of Being.* 2d ed. New York: Van Nostrand Reinhold.

Matson, Robert E. April 1963. "A Study of the Influence of Fraternity, Residence Hall, and Off-Campus Living on Students of High, Average, and Low College Potential." *Journal of NAWDAC* 26: 24–29.

Medsker, Leland L., and Tillery, Dale. 1971. *Breaking the Access Barriers.* New York: McGraw-Hill.

Merriam, Sharan, and Larry Mullins. 1981. "Havighurst's Adult Developmental Tasks: A Study of Their Importance Relative to Income, Age, and Sex." *Adult Education* 31: 123–41.

Messick, Samuel, and Associates. 1976. *Individuality in Learning.* San Francisco: Jossey-Bass.

Mezirow, Jack. 1981. "A Critical Theory of Adult Learning and Education." *Adult Education* 32: 3–24.

Miller, Richard I. 1979. *The Assessment of College Performance.* San Francisco: Jossey-Bass.

Miller, Theodore K., and Judith S. Prince. 1976. *The Future of Student Affairs.* San Francisco: Jossey-Bass.

Miller, Theodore K., Roger B. Winston, Jr., and William R. Mendenhall. 1983a. "Human Development and Higher Education." In *Administration and Leadership in Student Affairs,* edited by Theodore K. Miller, Roger B. Winston, Jr., and William R. Mendenhall. Muncie, Ind.: Accelerated Development.

———, eds. 1983b. *Administration and Leadership in Student Affairs.* Muncie, Ind.: Accelerated Development.

Miller, Thomas E. Summer 1986. "Commuter Issues at Small Institutions." *NASPA Journal* 24: 43–47.

Minkevich, George, Rickey L. George, and Jon C. Marshall. April/May 1972. "Personality Differences for Two- and Four-Year College Commuters." *College Student Journal* 6: 87–91.

Monroe, Charles R. 1972. *Profile of the Community College.* San Francisco: Jossey-Bass.

Moore, Betty L., Patricia C. Peterson, and Robert Wirag. 1984. "Orienting Traditional Entering Students." In *Orienting Students to College,* edited by M. Lee Upcraft. New Directions for Student Services No. 25. San Francisco: Jossey-Bass.

Moore, William, Jr. 1970. *Against the Odds.* San Francisco: Jossey-Bass.

Moos, Rudolf H. 1976. *The Human Context: Environmental Determinants of Behavior.* New York: Wiley-Interscience.

———. 1979. *Evaluating Educational Environments.* San Francisco: Jossey-Bass.

Morstain, Barry. April 1972. "The Importance of Student Interaction in the Freshman Year: Some Bases of an Experimental Living-Learning Program." *NASPA Journal* 9: 283–87.

Morstain, Barry R., and John C. Smart. 1977. "A Motivational Typology of Adult Learners." *Journal of Higher Education* 48: 665–79.

Mueller, Kate Hevner. 1961. *Student Personnel Work in Higher Education.* Cambridge, Mass.: Riverside Press.

Mussano, Frank. 1976. "The Effects of a Compulsory On-campus Residency Policy upon Academic Achievement for Freshmen." ED 129 378. 21 pp. MF–01; PC–01.

National Clearinghouse for Commuter Programs. 1987. *Commuter Students: References and Resources.* College Park, Md.: Author.

———. 1989. *Serving Commuter Students: Examples of Good Practice.* College Park, Md.: Author.

Neugarten, Bernice. 1975. "Adult Personality: Toward a Psychology of Life Cycle." In *The Human Life Cycle,* edited by W.C. Sze. New York: Jason Aronson.

———, ed. 1968. *Middle Age and Aging.* Chicago: Univ. of Chicago Press.

Newman, Barbara M., and Philip R. Newman. 1979. *Development through Life: A Psychosocial Approach.* Homewood, Ill.: Dorsey Press.

Newman, Frank. 1985. *Higher Education and the American Resur-*

gence. Princeton, N.J.: Carnegie Foundation for the Advancement of Teaching. ED 265 759. 282 pp. MF–01; PC not available EDRS.

Noel, Lee. 1985. "Increasing Student Retention: New Challenges and Potential." In *Increasing Student Retention,* edited by Lee Noel, Randi Levitz, Diana Saluri, and Associates. San Francisco: Jossey-Bass.

Noel, Lee, Randi Levitz, Diana Saluri, and Associates, eds. 1985. *Increasing Student Retention.* San Francisco: Jossey-Bass.

Novaco, Raymond W., Daniel Stokols, Joan Campbell, and Jeannette Stokols. 1979. "Transportation, Stress, and Community Psychology." *American Journal of Community Psychology* 7: 361–80.

Office of Student Life. Winter 1986. "Commuter Students: A Strong Academic, Vocational Orientation." Correspondence. Cincinnati: Univ. of Cincinnati.

———. 1986–87. "Developmental Tasks: A Comparison of Commuter to Residence Hall Students." Student Life Research Report No. 4. Cincinnati: Univ. of Cincinnati.

Pace, G. Robert, and George G. Stern. 1958. "An Approach to the Measurement of Psychological Characteristics of College Environments." *Journal of Educational Psychology* 49: 269–77.

Packwood, William T., ed. 1977. *College Student Personnel Services.* Springfield, Ill.: Charles C. Thomas.

Pantages, Timothy J., and Carol F. Creedon. 1978. "Studies of College Attrition: 1950–1975." *Review of Educational Research* 48: 49–101.

Parelius, Ann P. 1979. "Age Inequality in Educational Opportunity: The Needs of Adult Students in Higher Education." *Adult Education* 29: 180–93.

Parnell, Dale. 1985. *The Neglected Majority.* Washington, D.C.: Community College Press.

Pascarella, Ernest T. 1980. "Student-Faculty Informal Contact and College Outcomes." *Review of Educational Research* 50: 545–95.

———. 1984. "Reassessing the Effects of Living on Campus versus Commuting to College: A Causal Modeling Approach." *Review of Higher Education* 7: 247–60.

———. 1985a. "The Influence of On-campus Living versus Commuting to College on Intellectual and Interpersonal Self-Concept." *Journal of College Student Personnel* 26: 292–99.

———. 1985b. "Students' Affective Development within the College Environment." *Journal of Higher Education* 56: 640–63.

———, ed. 1982. *Studying Student Attrition.* New Directions for Institutional Research No. 36. San Francisco: Jossey-Bass.

Pascarella, Ernest T., Paul B. Duby, and Barbara K. Iverson. 1983. "A Test and Reconceptualization of a Theoretical Model of College Withdrawal in a Commuter Institutional Setting." *Sociology of Education* 56: 88–100.

Pascarella, Ernest T., Paul B. Duby, Vernon A. Miller, and Sue P.

Rasher. 1981. "Preenrollment Variables and Academic Performance as Predictors of Freshman Year Persistence, Early Withdrawal, and Stopout Behavior in an Urban, Nonresidential University." *Research in Higher Education* 15: 329–49.

Pascarella, Ernest T., Paul B. Duby, Patrick T. Terenzini, and Barbara K. Iverson. 1983. "Student-Faculty Relationships and Freshman Year Intellectual and Personal Growth in a Nonresidential Setting." *Journal of College Student Personnel* 24: 395–402.

Pascarella, Ernest T., and Patrick T. Terenzini. 1980. "Student-Faculty and Student-Peer Relationships as Mediators of the Structural Effects of Undergraduate Residence Arrangements." *Journal of Educational Research* 73: 344–53.

Pascarella, Ernest T., Patrick T. Terenzini, and Lee M. Wolfle. 1986. "Orientation to College and Freshman Year Persistence/Withdrawal Decisions." *Journal of Higher Education* 57: 155–75.

Penney, James F., and Delora E. Buckles. 1966. "Student Needs and Services on an Urban Campus." *Journal of College Student Personnel* 7: 180–85.

Perry, William, Jr. 1970. *Intellectual and Ethical Development in the College Years.* New York: Holt Rinehart & Winston.

Peterson, Marvin W., ed. 1987. *Key Resources on Higher Education, Governance, Management, and Leadership.* San Francisco: Jossey-Bass.

Peterson, Nancy A. 1975. "Commuting Student Lacks Advantages of Dorm Resident." Minneapolis: Univ. of Minnesota, Center for Educational Development. ED 122 720. 13 pp. MF–01; PC–01.

Peterson, Richard E. 1965. "On a Typology of College Students." ETS Report No. RB-65-9. Princeton, N.J.: Educational Testing Service.

Phillips, John. 1981. "Theory, Practice, and Basic Beliefs in Adult Education." *Adult Education* 31: 93–106.

Prusok, Ralph E. 1960. "The Off-campus Student." *Journal of College Student Personnel* 2: 2–9.

Prusok, Ralph E., and W. Bruce Walsh. 1964. "College Students' Residence and Academic Achievement." *Journal of College Student Personnel* 5: 180–84.

Pugh, Richard C., and Phillip C. Chamberlain. 1976. "Undergraduate Residence: An Assessment of Academic Achievement in a Predominantly University Community." *Journal of College Student Personnel* 17: 138–41.

Reeve, J.T. 1966. "The Commuter—An Intriguing Phenomenon." In *The ACU-I Proceedings of the 43rd Annual Conference:* 136–41. Ithaca, N.Y.: Cornell Univ.

Reichard, Donald J., and Patricia P. McArver. 1975. "Demographic Characteristics of Commuting Students." Greensboro: Univ. of North Carolina at Greensboro, Office of Institutional Research. ED 119 599. 25 pp. MF–01; PC–01.

Reisman, Betty L., Mary Lawless, Rosemary Robinson, and Joanne Beckett. 1983. "Urban Graduate Students: A Need for Community." *College Student Journal* 17: 48–50.

Rhatigan, James J. Summer 1986. "Developing a Campus Profile of Commuting Students." *NASPA Journal* 24: 4–10.

Richardson, Richard C., Jr., and Louis W. Bender. 1985. *Students in Urban Settings: Achieving the Baccalaureate Degree.* ASHE-ERIC Higher Education Report No. 6. Washington, D.C.: Association for the Study of Higher Education. ED 265 798. 90 pp. MF–01; PC–04.

Richmond, Jayne. 1986. "The Importance of Student Involvement: A Dialogue with Alexander Astin." *Journal of Counseling and Development* 65: 92–95.

Riesman, David, and Christopher Jencks. 1962. "The Viability of the American College." In *The American College,* edited by Nevitt Sanford. New York: John Wiley & Sons.

Rodgers, Robert F. 1980. "Theories Underlying Student Development." In *Student Development in Higher Education: Theories, Practices, and Future Directions,* edited by Don G. Creamer. ACPA Media Publication No.27. Alexandria, Va.: American College Personnel Association.

Roe, Ann. 1957. "Early Determinants of Vocational Choice." *Journal of Counseling Psychology* 4: 212–17.

Rosenberg, Morris, and B. Claire McCullough. 1981. "Mattering: Inferred Significance and Mental Health among Adolescents." In *Research in Community and Mental Health,* vol. 2, edited by R. Simmons. Greenwich, Conn.: JAI Press.

Rudolph, Frederick. 1962. *The American College and University.* New York: Knopf.

Rue, Penny, and Sylvia Stewart. April 1982. "Toward a Definition of the Commuter Student Population in Higher Education." *NASPA Forum* 2: 8–9.

Ryan, James T. January 1970. "College Freshmen and Living Arrangements." *NASPA Journal* 7: 127–30.

Sanford, Nevitt. 1966. *Self and Society.* New York: Atherton.

———, ed. 1962. *The American College.* New York: John Wiley & Sons.

Sauber, S. Richard. 1972. "College Adjustment and Place of Residence." *Journal of College Student Personnel* 13: 205–8.

Schein, Howard K., Ned Scott Laff, and Deborah R. Allen. 1987. *Giving Advice to Students: A Road Map for College Professionals.* ACPA Media Publication No. 44. Alexandria, Va.: American College Personnel Association.

Schlossberg, Nancy K. 1981. "A Model for Analyzing Human Adaptation to Transition." *The Counseling Psychologist* 9(2): 2–18.

———. 1984. *Counseling Adults in Transition: Linking Practice with Theory.* New York: Springer.

————. 1985. "Marginality and Mattering: A Life Span Approach." Paper presented at a meeting of the American Psychological Association, Los Angeles, California.

Schlossberg, Nancy K., Ann Q. Lynch, and Arthur W. Chickering. 1989. *Improving Higher Education Environments for Adults*. San Francisco: Jossey-Bass.

Schneider, Lynette Daniels. 1977. "Housing." In *College Student Personnel Services,* edited by William T. Packwood. Springfield, Ill.: Charles C. Thomas.

Schotzinger, Kay A., Jim Buchanan, and William F. Fahrenbach. Winter 1976. "Nonresidence Advisors: A Peer Counseling Program for Commuter Students." *NASPA Journal* 13: 42–46.

Schuchman, Herman P. 1966. "The Double Life of the Commuter College Student." *Mental Hygiene* 50: 104–10.

————. 1974. "Special Tasks of Commuter Students." *Personnel and Guidance Journal* 52: 465–70.

Sedlacek, William E., Glenwood C. Brooks, Jr., Javier Miyares, and Mark W. Hardwick. 1976. "A Comparison of Black and White University Student Commuters." *Journal of College Student Personnel* 17: 134–37.

Segal, Stanley J. 1967. "Implications of Residential Setting for Development during College." *Journal of College Student Personnel* 8: 308–10.

Seppanen, Loretta J. Autumn 1981. "Improving Community College Advising Systems." *NASPA Journal* 19: 39–44.

Shaffer, Robert H. 1959. "Effect of Large Enrollments on Student Personnel Services." *Personnel and Guidance Journal:* 626–32.

Shriberg, Arthur. Spring 1984. "A Self-Audit: Preparing for the Adult Learner." *NASPA Journal* 21: 24–27.

————, ed. 1980. *Providing Student Services for the Adult Learner.* New Directions for Student Services No. 11. San Francisco: Jossey-Bass.

Simono, R.B., Dale Wachowiak, and Susan R. Furr. Summer 1984. "Student Living Arrangements and Their Perceived Impact on Academic Performance: A Brief Follow-up." *Journal of College and University Student Housing* 14: 22–24.

Slade, Irving L., and Lore Jarmul. Spring 1975. "Commuting College Students: The Neglected Majority." *College Board Review* 95: 16–20.

Smith, Laurence N., Ronald Lippitt, Lee Noel, and Dorian Sprandel. 1981. *Mobilizing the Campus for Retention: An Innovative Quality-of-Life Model.* Iowa City: American College Testing Program.

Spratt, Patricia A. Spring 1984. "Needs and Interests of Adult Learners: What Do They Seek on a Campus?" *NASPA Journal* 21: 4–8.

Stark, Matthew. 1965. "Commuter and Residence Hall Students Compared." *Personnel and Guidance Journal* 44: 277–81.

Steltenpohl, Elizabeth, and Jane Shipton. 1986. "Facilitating a Successful Transition to College for Adults." *Journal of Higher Education* 57: 637–58.

Stern, G.G. 1970. *People in Context.* New York: John Wiley & Sons.

Stewart, Sylvia S. 1985. "Students Who Commute." In *Increasing Student Retention,* edited by Lee Noel, Randi Levitz, Diana Saluri, and Associates. San Francisco: Jossey-Bass.

———, ed. 1983. *Commuter Students: Enhancing Their Educational Experiences.* New Directions for Student Services No. 24. San Francisco: Jossey-Bass.

Stewart, Sylvia S., and Penny Rue. 1983. "Commuter Students: Definition and Distribution." In *Commuter Students: Enhancing Their Educational Experiences,* edited by Sylvia S. Stewart. New Directions for Student Services No. 24. San Francisco: Jossey-Bass.

Stodt, Martha M. Spring 1982. "Psychological Characteristics of 1980's College Students: Continuity, Changes, and Challenges." *NASPA Journal* 19: 3–8.

Stodt, Martha McGinty, and William M. Klepper, eds. 1987. *Increasing Retention: Academic and Student Affairs Administrators in Partnership.* New Directions for Higher Education No. 60. San Francisco: Jossey-Bass.

Stokols, Daniel, and Raymond W. Novaco. 1981. "Transportation and Well-Being." In *Transportation and Behavior,* edited by Irwin Altman, Joachim F. Wohlwill, and Peter B. Everett. New York: Plenum Press.

Stokols, Daniel, Raymond W. Novaco, Jeannette Stokols, and Joan Campbell. 1978. "Traffic Congestion, Type A Behavior, and Stress." *Journal of Applied Psychology* 63: 467–80.

Study Group on the Conditions of Excellence in American Higher Education. 1984. *Involvement in Higher Learning: Realizing the Potential of American Higher Education.* Washington, D.C.: National Institute of Education.

Suddick, David E., and Lee Owens. Spring 1982. "The Adult College Student: What Developmental Education Services Do They Desire?" *College Student Journal* 16: 89–91.

Sullivan, Kenneth, and Anne Sullivan. 1980. "Adolescent-Parent Separation." *Developmental Psychology* 16: 93–99.

Task Group on General Education. 1988. *A New Vitality in General Education.* Washington, D.C.: Association of American Colleges. ED 290 387. 64 pp. MF–01; PC not available EDRS.

Teahan, John E. 1963. "Parental Attitudes and College Success." *Journal of Educational Psychology* 54: 104–9.

Thomas, Russell, and Arthur W. Chickering. 1984. "Education and Identity Revisited." *Journal of College Student Personnel* 25: 392–99.

Thon, Andrew J. Spring 1984. "Responding to the Nonacademic Needs of Adult Students." *NASPA Journal* 21: 28–35.

Tinto, Vincent. 1987. *Leaving College.* Chicago: Univ. of Chicago Press.

Titus, Chester R. 1972. "Students Express Their Housing Needs and Preferences." *Journal of College Student Personnel* 13: 202–4.

U.S. Department of Education. June 1988. *The National Postsecondary Student Aid Study.* Washington, D.C.: Center for Education Statistics.

United Way of America. 1987. *What Lies Ahead? Looking toward the '90s.* Alexandria, Va.: Author.

Upcraft, M. Lee, ed. 1984. *Orienting Students to College.* New Directions for Student Services No. 25. San Francisco: Jossey-Bass.

Urban Community Colleges Commission. 1988. *Minorities in Urban Community Colleges.* Washington, D.C.: American Association of Community and Junior Colleges.

Vaillant, G.E. 1977. *Adaptation to Life.* Boston: Little, Brown & Co.

Valverde, Leonard A. 1985. "Low-Income Students." In *Increasing Student Retention,* edited by Lee Noel, Randi Levitz, Diana Saluri, and Associates. San Francisco: Jossey-Bass.

Velez, William. 1985. "Finishing College: The Effects of College Type." *Sociology of Education* 58: 191–200.

Walker, E.T. 1935. "Student Housing and University Success." *School and Society* 42: 575–77.

Walsh, Bruce W., and Nancy E. Betz. 1985. *Tests and Assessment.* Englewood Cliffs, N.J.: Prentice-Hall.

Walsh, Norma, ed. 1982. *Normal Family Processes.* New York: Guilford Press.

Ward, R.F., and T.E. Kurz. 1969. *The Commuting Student: A Study of Facilities at Wayne State University.* ED 031 901. 39 pp. MF–01; PC–02.

Warren, William H, ed. 1986. *Improving Institutional Services to Adult Learners.* Washington, D.C.: American Council on Education.

Weiner, Bernard. 1979. "A Theory of Motivation for Some Classroom Experiences." *Journal of Educational Psychology* 71: 3–25.

Welty, John D. 1976. "Resident and Commuter Students: Is It Only the Living Situation?" *Journal of College Student Personnel*: 465–68.

Wheaton, Janilee B., and Daniel C. Robinson. Winter 1983. "Responding to the Needs of Reentry Women: A Comprehensive Campus Model." *NASPA Journal* 21: 44–51.

White, Carla J. Spring 1984. "Adult Student Support Groups on the Campus." *NASPA Journal* 21: 55–58.

Widick, Carole, Lee Knefelkamp, and Clyde A. Parker. 1980. "Student Development." In *Student Services: A Handbook for the Profession,* edited by Ursula Delworth, Gary Hanson, and Associates. San Francisco: Jossey-Bass.

Willett, Lynn H. 1985. "Life-Style Variables Related to Community

College Attendance." *Community/Junior College* 9: 281–89.

Williamson, E.G., and Donald A. Biggs. 1975. *Student Personnel Work: A Program of Developmental Relationships.* New York: John Wiley & Sons.

Wills, Byron S., and James J. Ross. Summer 1976. "Food Service and Residence Hall Facilities Being Offered to Commuters by Member Institutions of ACUHO." *Journal of College and University Student Housing* 6: 13–16.

Wilmes, Martha Baer, and Stephanie L. Quade. Summer 1986. "Perspectives on Programming for Commuters: Examples of Good Practice." *ASPA Journal* 24: 25–35.

Wilson, Richard J., Stephen A. Anderson, and William Michael Fleming. 1987. "Commuter and Resident Students' Personal and Family Adjustment." *Journal of College Student Personnel* 28: 229–33.

Wolfgang, Mary E., and William D. Dowling. 1981. "Differences in Motivation of Adult and Younger Undergraduates." *Journal of Higher Education* 52: 640–48.

Wright, Doris J. 1987a. "Minority Students: Developmental Beginnings." In *Responding to the Needs of Today's Minority Students,* edited by Doris J. Wright. New Directions for Student Services No. 38. San Francisco: Jossey-Bass.

————, ed. 1987b. *Responding to the Needs of Today's Minority Students.* New Directions for Student Services No. 38. San Francisco: Jossey-Bass.

INDEX

A

Academic advising, 53
Academic program selection, 46
Academic success, 17-18
Accessibility, 58
Accommodation approach, 11-12
Acculturation, 30
Action plan development, 64-66
Administrators
    attitudes, 12-13
    leadership role, 62-65
    staff role in environment, 50
Admissions
    practices, 62, 63
    staff, 50-51
Adult development theory, 30
Adult students
    equitable services, 49
    increasing numbers, 2, 24
    involvement, 38
African-American students, 3
Age
    categorization, 4
    research question, 43
    traditional students, 2, 39
American College Personnel Association, 23
American College Testing Program, 46
American Council on Education, 3
American Indian students, 3
Animal House, 11
Articulation policy, 50, 51
Asian students, 3
Astin studies, 17, 22
Attitudes, 12-13
Attrition: high risk, 1

B

Belonging
    basic need, 36
    developing sense of 6
    institutional environment, 54-55, 60
"Blue shirt institution," 19
Breaking Away, 11

C

Campus ecology, 34-35
Career planning, 53
Categorization, 4, 5

D

Data collection, 59, 65
Development officers, 50
Diversity of students
       desired "mix," 50
       trends, 2-4
       research on, 23-24
Dormitory concept, 10
Dropouts
       and involvement, 22
       living arrangements, 18
       process, 38
       research on, 60

E

Ecosystem model, 34-35
Education Commission of the States, 27
Education reform reports, 26-28
Educational Facilities Laboratories, 23
Ego development, 32
Employment
       campus jobs, 55, 64
       effect, 60
       student status, 44
Enrollment trends
       diversity, 2-4
       growth, 10
Environment
       assessment, 49-59
       college, 32, 59
       -person "fit," 33-34
"Equity" institutional response stage, 63-64
Erickson theory, 31-32
Esteem, 36
Ethnic background
       "new" students, 24
       research question, 43
Evening students, 12, 49
Extracurricular activities (see Cocurricular activities)

F

Facilities, 58
Faculty
       attitudes, 12-13
       composition, 54
       -student interaction, 52, 53-54, 60, 66
Family
       campus activities, 51

N

NASPA Journal, 25
National Clearinghouse for Commuter Programs (NCCP), 23, 46
Needs (see Student needs)
Negative assumptions
    perpetuation, 20–21
    research images, 17
New Directions for Student Services, 25
A New Vitality in General Education, 27
Not to Eat, Not for Love, 11

O

Ohio State University, 26
Older students (see Adult students)
Orientation programs, 51–52, 56, 63
Outreach, 56
Overnight accommodations, 58

P

Parent education level, 43
Parking, 5, 12, 58
Part-time students
    commuter categorization, 4
    equitable services, 49
    increasing numbers, 2, 3
    research question, 43
Peer advisors, 53
Perry theory, 32–33
Persistence, 37
Person-environment "fit," 33–34
Physiological needs, 36
Political issues, 64–65
Preservationist attitude, 11
Princeton University, 10
Psychosocial theory, 31–32
Public relations staff, 50
Publications: institutional, 49–50, 62, 63

R

Recreation facilities, 58
Recruitment, 62, 63
Reentry students (see Adult students)
Remedial aid, 46, 53
Research
    applicability of models, 29
    data availability, 46
    gaps in, 14–15

Two year colleges (see Community colleges)

U

University of Chicago, 10
University of Cincinnati, 26
University of Maryland at College Park, 23, 26
Urban institutions
    approaches, 12
    commuter students, 1
    student diversity, 3, 24

V

Values
    institutional, 64–65
    student, 34
Veterans, 55

W

Weekend students, 12
Weller, 11
Withdrawal (see Dropouts)
Women students
    increasing numbers, 3
    support groups, 55
World War I, 10
World War II, 10

ASHE-ERIC HIGHER EDUCATION REPORTS

Since 1983, the Association for the Study of Higher Education (ASHE) and the Educational Resources Information Center (ERIC) Clearinghouse on Higher Education, a sponsored project of the School of Education and Human Development at The George Washington University, have cosponsored the *ASHE-ERIC Higher Education Report* series. The 1989 series is the eighteenth overall and the first to be published by the School of Education and Human Development at the George Washington University.

Each monograph is the definitive analysis of a tough higher education problem, based on thorough research of pertinent literature and insitutional experiences. Topics are identified by a national survey. Noted practitioners and scholars are then commissioned to write the reports, with experts providing critical reviews of each manuscript before publication.

Eight monographs (10 before 1985) in the ASHE-ERIC Higher Education Report series are published each year and are available on a individual or subscription basis. Subscription to eight issues is $80.00 annually; $60 to members of AAHE, AIR, or AERA; and $50 to ASHE members. All foreign subscribers must include an additional $10 per series year for postage.

Prices for single copies, including book rate postage, are $15.00 regular and $11.25 for members of AERA, AIR, AAHE, and ASHE ($10.00 regular and $7.50 for members for 1985 to 1987 reports, $7.50 regular and $6.00 for members for 1983 and 1984 reports, $6.50 regular and $5.00 for members for reports published before 1982). All foreign orders must include $1.00 per book for foreign postage. Fast United Parcel Service or first class postage is available for $1.00 per book in the U.S. and $2.50 per book outside the U.S. (orders above $50.00 may substitute 5% of the total invoice amount for domestic postage). Make checks payable to ASHE-ERIC. For VISA and MasterCard payments, include card number, expiration date, and signature. Orders under $25 must be prepaid. Bulk discounts are available on orders of 15 or more reports (not applicable to subscription orders). Order from the Publications Department, ASHE-ERIC Higher Education Reports, The George Washington University, One Dupont Circle, Suite 630, Washington, DC 20036-1183, or phone us at (202) 296-2597. Write for a complete catalog of all available reports.

1989 ASHE-ERIC Higher Education Reports

1. Making Sense of Administrative Leadership: The 'L' Word in Higher Education
   Estela M. Bensimon, Anna Neumann, and Robert Birnbaum

2. Affirmative Rhetoric, Negative Action: African-American and Hispanic Faculty at Predominantly White Universities
   Valora Washington and William Harvey

3. Postsecondary Developmental Programs: A Traditional Agenda with New Imperatives
   Louise M. Tomlinson

4. The Old College Try: Balancing Athletics and Academics in Higher Education
   John R. Thelin and Lawrence L. Wiseman

5. The Challenge of Diversity: Involvement or Alienation in the Academy?
   Daryl G. Smith

6. Student Goals for College and Courses: A Missing Link in Assessing and Improving Academic Achievement
   Joan S. Stark, Kathleen M. Shaw, and Malcolm A. Lowther

1988 ASHE-ERIC Higher Education Reports

1. The Invisible Tapestry: Culture in American Colleges and Universities
   George D. Kuh and Elizabeth J. Whitt

2. Critical Thinking: Theory, Research, Practice, and Possibilities
   Joanne Gainen Kurfiss

3. Developing Academic Programs: The Climate for Innovation
   Daniel T. Seymour

4. Peer Teaching: To Teach is To Learn Twice
   Neal A. Whitman

5. Higher Education and State Governments: Renewed Partnership, Cooperation, or Competition?
   Edward R. Hines

6. Entrepreneurship and Higher Education: Lessons for Colleges, Universities, and Industry
   James S. Fairweather

7. Planning for Microcomputers in Higher Education: Strategies for the Next Generation
   Reynolds Ferrante, John Hayman, Mary Susan Carlson, and Harry Phillips

8. The Challenge for Research in Higher Education: Harmonizing Excellence and Utility
   Alan W. Lindsay and Ruth T. Neumann

1987 ASHE-ERIC Higher Education Reports

1. Incentive Early Retirement Programs for Faculty: Innovative Responses to a Changing Environment
   Jay L. Chronister and Thomas R. Kepple, Jr.

2. Working Effectively with Trustees: Building Cooperative Campus Leadership
   Barbara E. Taylor

3. Formal Recognition of Employer-Sponsored Instruction: Conflict and Collegiality in Postsecondary Education
   Nancy S. Nash and Elizabeth M. Hawthorne

4. Learning Styles: Implications for Improving Educational Practices
   Charles S. Claxton and Patricia H. Murrell

5. Higher Education Leadership: Enhancing Skills through Professional Development Programs
   Sharon A. McDade

6. Higher Education and the Public Trust: Improving Stature in Colleges and Universities
   Richard L. Alfred and Julie Weissman

7. College Student Outcomes Assessment: A Talent Development Perspective
   Maryann Jacobi, Alexander Astin, and Frank Ayala, Jr.

8. Opportunity from Strength: Strategic Planning Clarified with Case Examples
   Robert G. Cope

1986 ASHE-ERIC Higher Education Reports

1. Post-tenure Faculty Evaluation: Threat or Opportunity?
   Christine M. Licata

2. Blue Ribbon Commissions and Higher Education: Changing Academe from the Outside
   Janet R. Johnson and Laurence R. Marcus

3. Responsive Professional Education: Balancing Outcomes and Opportunities
   Joan S. Stark, Malcolm A. Lowther, and Bonnie M.K. Hagerty

4. Increasing Students' Learning: A Faculty Guide to Reducing Stress among Students
   Neal A. Whitman, David C. Spendlove, and Claire H. Clark

5. Student Financial Aid and Women: Equity Dilemma?
   Mary Moran

6. The Master's Degree: Tradition, Diversity, Innovation
   Judith S. Glazer

7. The College, the Constitution, and the Consumer Student: Implications for Policy and Practice
   Robert M. Hendrickson and Annette Gibbs

8. Selecting College and University Personnel: The Quest and the Question
   Richard A. Kaplowitz

1985 ASHE-ERIC Higher Education Reports

1. Flexibility in Academic Staffing: Effective Policies and Practices
   Kenneth P. Mortimer, Marque Bagshaw, and Andrew T. Masland

2. Associations in Action: The Washington, D.C. Higher Education Community
   Harland G. Bloland

3. And on the Seventh Day: Faculty Consulting and Supplemental Income
   Carol M. Boyer and Darrell R. Lewis

4. Faculty Research Performance: Lessons from the Sciences and Social Sciences
   John W. Creswell

5. Academic Program Review: Institutional Approaches, Expectations, and Controversies
   Clifton F. Conrad and Richard F. Wilson

6. Students in Urban Settings: Achieving the Baccalaureate Degree
   Richard C. Richardson, Jr. and Louis W. Bender

7. Serving More Than Students: A Critical Need for College Student Personnel Services
   Peter H. Garland

8. Faculty Participation in Decision Making: Necessity or Luxury?
   Carol E. Floyd

1984 ASHE-ERIC Higher Education Reports

1. Adult Learning: State Policies and Institutional Practices
   K. Patricia Cross and Anne-Marie McCartan

2. Student Stress: Effects and Solutions
   Neal A. Whitman, David C. Spendlove, and Claire H. Clark

3. Part-time Faulty: Higher Education at a Crossroads
   Judith M. Gappa

4. Sex Discrimination Law in Higher Education: The Lessons of the Past Decade
   J. Ralph Lindgren, Patti T. Ota, Perry A. Zirkel, and Nan Van Gieson

5. Faculty Freedoms and Institutional Accountability: Interactions and Conflicts
   Steven G. Olswang and Barbara A. Lee

6. The High Technology Connection: Academic/Industrial Cooperation for Economic Growth
   Lynn G. Johnson

7. Employee Educational Programs: Implications for Industry and Higher Education
   Suzanne W. Morse

8. Academic Libraries: The Changing Knowledge Centers of Colleges and Universities
   Barbara B. Moran

9. Futures Research and the Strategic Planning Process: Implications for Higher Education
   James L. Morrison, William L. Renfro, and Wayne I. Boucher

10. Faculty Workload: Research, Theory, and Interpretation
    Harold E. Yuker

1983 ASHE-ERIC Higher Education Reports

1. The Path to Excellence: Quality Assurance in Higher Education
   Laurence R. Marcus, Anita O. Leone, and Edward D. Goldberg

2. Faculty Recruitment, Retention, and Fair Employment: Obligations and Opportunities
   John S. Waggaman

3. Meeting the Challenges: Developing Faculty Careers*
   Michael C.T. Brooks and Katherine L. German

4. Raising Academic Standards: A Guide to Learning Improvement
   Ruth Talbott Keimig

5. Serving Learners at a Distance: A Guide to Program Practices
   Charles E. Feasley

6. Competence, Admissions, and Articulation: Returning to the Basics in Higher Education
   Jean L. Preer

7. Public Service in Higher Education: Practices and Priorities
   Patricia H. Crosson

8. Academic Employment and Retrenchment: Judicial Review and Administrative Action
   Robert M. Hendrickson and Barbara A. Lee

9. Burnout: The New Academic Disease*
   Winifred Albizu Meléndez and Rafael M. de Guzmán

10. Academic Workplace: New Demands, Heightened Tensions
    Ann E. Austin and Zelda F. Gamson

*Out-of-print. Available through EDRS. Call 1-800-227-ERIC.